The Easy Way
to Artisan Breads & Pastries

Designed by Michel Opatowski
Edited by Phyllis Glazer
Food styling by Natasha Haimovich

Library of Congress Cataloging-in-Publication Data

Laskin, Avner.
    The easy way to artisan breads & pastries / Avner Laskin; photography by Josef Salis.
        p. cm.
    Includes index.
    ISBN 1-4027-1260-X
    1. Bread. 2. Baking. I. Title.

TX769.L277 2004
641.8'15—dc22

2004056591

10 9 8 7 6 5 4 3 2 1

Published by Sterling Publishing Co., Inc.
387 Park Avenue South, New York, NY 10016
© 2005 by Penn Publishing
Distributed in Canada by Sterling Publishing
c/o Canadian Manda Group, 165 Dufferin Street
Toronto, Ontario, Canada M6K 3H6
Distributed in Great Britain by Chrysalis Books Group PLC
The Chrysalis Building, Bramley Road, London W10 6SP, England
Distributed in Australia by Capricorn Link (Australia) Pty. Ltd.
P.O. Box 704, Windsor, NSW 2756, Australia

Printed in China

Sterling ISBN 1-4027-1260-X

The Easy Way to Artisan Breads & Pastries

AVNER LASKIN

Photography by JOSEF SALIS

Sterling Publishing Co., Inc.
New York

Contents

Introduction

Bread. The very word conjures up all kinds of sensually pleasing associations for me. Through my studies in France and travels around the world, I've learned to bake hundreds of different kinds of breads and pastries. But the fact that simple ingredients like water and flour can be turned into a marvelous loaf of fresh bread still seems like magic to me.

When I was growing up bread, was never thrown out. If it passed its prime my mother toasted it or turned it into bread crumbs, bread pudding, or French toast. And if there were any leftover crumbs, my father fed them to the neighborhood birds!

Right next door, my neighbors had their own ingenious ways to use stale bread, like in Italian *panzanella* salad or Lebanese *fattoush*.

A collection of my favorite recipes, this book is designed for those of you who enjoy the artistry and magic involved in the creation of handmade breads, without the humdrum taste and artificial additives usually present in commercial loaves. As you glance through the pages, you'll find a tempting selection of delicious breads and baked goods from around the world, all baked in my own home kitchen under standard conditions. As a professional baker, the greatest challenge for me was to turn complicated recipes into ones that would be easy and clear enough for any home baker but still ensure professional results. That means I've found ways to create the same breads for which famous bakers require commercial ovens right in your own home oven!

You might be surprised to discover that you don't have to be an artisan to make artisan breads. In fact, the recipes in this book even take the guesswork out of kneading. Instead of wondering if you've kneaded sufficiently to create the right texture, all you need to do is use a sturdy standing electric mixer with a dough hook and follow the exact kneading times indicated in the recipes. Contrary to popular opinion, an electric mixer will always yield a better-textured bread, especially one with high-gluten flours, provided that the kneading is correctly timed so that the gluten will reach the proper height.

Once you've passed the beginner's phase, why not try one recipe using a fermented dough that adds depth to both taste and texture? The Germans have more than eight common varieties of fermented doughs, called "sours" (like our sourdough starters in America); the Italians use *biga*; and the French, *sponge* or *poolish*. Their preparation is more time-consuming, but the results are definitely worth it.

Bread is a fascinating complex of textures and chemical reactions, incorporating history, tradition, and culture. From the soft English white bread to crispy Italian flatbreads, from goodies like Italian and French morning pastries to the classic babka, you'll find a world of flavors to choose from in this book. I hope you'll find as much fun and enjoyment in baking these artisan breads and pastries as I have had in preparing them for you.

Avner Laskin

The Baker's Tools

*In this book we'll be doing all our mixing and kneading with a **standing electric mixer** using a dough hook. I recommend using semi-professional (or professional) models with a powerful motor (at least 800 watts).*

Set of glass bowls. You'll need the standard sizes, but make sure to have an especially large, wide bowl for rising.

Kitchen towels. The best kitchen towels for bread baking are 50% cotton and 50% linen, like those used in France. In addition to other kitchen tasks, we'll be using them as a rising surface and as a (floured) liner for a rising bowl. (A cloth towel is used to cover rising dough when we want it to breathe, rather than sweat, as it would if covered with plastic wrap.)

Good *sharp knife* to make slashes.

Pastry brush for brushing the loaves.

Rolling pin. Always flour the rolling pin.

Work surface. While many people work on a wooden board, I prefer to work on my marble countertop (especially with pastries) because the surface is colder.

A reliable *kitchen scale.*

Measuring cups & spoons.

A good *kitchen timer.*

A wooden *pizza paddle.*

The Baker's Pantry: Raw Materials

Flours

Although wheat flour is the major ingredient in virtually all types of breads and pastries, other grains are sometimes used to enhance both flavor and texture. In this book, we'll be using the following types of flour:

Barley flour was the first flour used to bake bread in ancient times. Low in protein, it results in a denser, coarser loaf, which is why it is always mixed with wheat flour in bread doughs. It is available in health food stores.

Bread flour is made from hard wheat and has a higher percentage of gluten than regular flour. This gives the dough more elasticity and lightness.

Cornmeal is most often used in American quick, non-yeast breads and should always be mixed with bread flour. It adds a crispy consistency to bread.

Durum, the hardest of all wheat varieties, has a yellow endosperm that gives dough a golden hue. It is often used in the production of premium pastas due to its high protein and gluten content.

Organic flour gives a slightly yellowish tinge to bread and greatly enriches its taste, but always check the package to make sure it has a protein content of over 12%. Organic flour may be substituted in any recipe that calls for wheat flour.

Semi-dark flour is used as the basis of French sourdough starter and produces a lighter loaf than whole wheat flour. Since this type of flour is not available in supermarkets, I use a combination of 2 parts *bread flour* plus 1 part *whole rye flour* plus 1 part *whole wheat flour*. In the recipes you'll see this combination spelled out rather than the term "semi-dark flour."

Unbleached all-purpose white flour is the standard type available in supermarkets.

Whole rye flour adds a distinctive flavor to various loaves. Because it inhibits gluten development, rye flour is always mixed with other types of flours in baking. It is also used to make sourdough starter.

Whole wheat flour adds flavor and nutrients but will result in a denser loaf. I recommend using stoneground whole wheat flour, which is made from the entire wheat kernel with nothing removed.

Cereals, Fiber & Seeds

Coriander seeds are used in small amounts to help enhance the flavor of breads. Like fennel or anise seeds, coriander seeds are considered a digestive aid.

Fennel seeds have an aniselike flavor that complements the taste of bread. They also aid digestion.

Flax seeds help lower cholesterol and add flavor to breads. Always store these seeds in the refrigerator.

Oatmeal adds rich flavor and texture to bread. A little oatmeal also aids sourdough starter activity.

Poppy seeds are rich in nutrients and are a popular garnish for breads and pastries. For use in cakes, ground poppy seeds are best. Store them in the refrigerator.

Pumpkin seeds add a nutlike taste and nutritional benefits to various breads, muffins, and other baked goods. Toasting them lightly in a dry frying pan or in the oven will enhance their aroma.

Sesame seeds are one of the most popular garnishes on bread and baked goods, especially in the Middle East and Mediterranean countries. Toasting the seeds lightly in a dry frying pan greatly enriches their flavor.

Wheat bran is the outer husk that encloses the wheat kernel. It is often added to bread dough to create a heartier texture, while the fiber aids digestion.

Wheat germ, the seed of the wheat plant, is rich in B vitamins and vitamin E. The addition of wheat germ to yeast dough not only enhances nutritional value but also helps develop the dough. Always store wheat germ in the refrigerator.

Liquid Ingredients & Enrichments

Beer gives an added "lift" to yeast, much like it does to those who drink it. It also enriches flavor. Even if it doesn't appear in a recipe, you can substitute up to 10% of the liquids called for with beer. Use light beers with recipes calling for all-purpose or bread flours, and dark beers in rye, whole wheat, and country-style breads.

Butter improves the taste and aroma of breads. Like eggs, butter also gives breads a soft, tender crumb and cakelike consistency. Melted butter is usually added at the beginning of the kneading process, while room-temperature butter is added toward the end.

Eggs enrich the taste of breads. The recipes in this book use large eggs.

Milk can replace water to give breads a more tender crumb. Brushing the loaf with milk before baking helps firm the crust and gives it a golden color. Always use full-fat (never low-fat) milk.

Olive oil adds a rich taste and golden tone to the bread.

Red wine can be substituted for up to 40% of the liquids in bread dough recipes, as the French like to do (of course!), especially when baking whole wheat and country-style breads. For best results, avoid using cooking wines; use only those that you wouldn't hesitate to drink.

Sunflower seed oil is one of the light, neutral oils I like to add to bread dough in small amounts to achieve an especially smooth texture with a soft, tender crumb.

Water, like flour, is one of the most basic bread dough ingredients. Since we'll be kneading with an electric mixer for all the recipes in this book, we'll also be using cold water. The extended kneading process will warm the dough anyway.

Like flour, liquids are fundamental to bread making, turning flour into dough. They not only activate yeast but also affect the texture of the finished product. Ingredients like eggs and fats are considered enriching ingredients because they change the character of simple flour-water-yeast dough in special ways. Use fats lke butter or oil, for example, to enrich the taste of breads. Bread bakers should be aware, however, that eggs and fats slow down fermentation and rising time.

The Magic of Yeast & Fermentation

Like a seed, yeast has the magical potential to give forth life stored within it. Add water, and it turns into a living organism that converts the natural sugars in flour to gases. These gases become trapped within the strands of gluten (protein) in the flour, making the bread rise. But there are other ways to make bread rise as well. Long before the discovery of yeast, ancient bakers used sourdough starter or "old dough" from a previous batch.

**TO SUBSTITUTE
FRESH YEAST FOR DRY YEAST:**

1 *teaspoon* dry yeast =
1/2 ounce fresh yeast.

1 *tablespoon* dry yeast =
11/2 ounces fresh yeast.

Using yeast There are two basic varieties of yeast available: fresh and dry. Fresh yeast is more delicate and somewhat more aromatic. Sold in the refrigerator section, fresh yeast is more difficult to find but worth looking for (especially for those recipes in which I particularly recommend it). Fresh yeast can be stored in the refrigerator for up to 2 weeks; it should be disposed of when the corners blacken and dry out.

Dry yeast is available in sachets and/or bulk packaging in every grocery store and supermarket. Some types recommend activating in lukewarm water before adding to the flour, but in my recipes I add it directly to the flour, where it is activated by the addition of liquids.

Fermented dough For centuries in many countries throughout the world, a piece of old dough has been used as a flavoring agent, like a spice. It doesn't have to be really old though; a 24- to 72-hour sojourn in the refrigerator is quite enough.

To make fermented dough, start with plain bread dough (only) and wrap 1/4- to 1/2-pound pieces loosely, first in greaseproof paper and then in foil, allowing room for the dough to expand. Let stand 24 hours in the refrigerator before using, or freeze for up to 6 months and defrost at room temperature.

Sponge starter Sponge starter is a batterlike combination of similar amounts of flour and water, plus a small amount of yeast, that is set aside for a few hours to ferment. Sponge starter results in a lighter bread with a less yeasty flavor. There are many different kinds of sponges, including poolish and biga.

Poolish The French version of sponge.

Biga Made with flour, water, and a small amount of yeast, biga is the Italian version of sponge starter, traditionally fermented for a minimum of 12 hours. Bread made with biga will have a lightly fermented taste and an open texture.

All About Sourdough

Basic Sourdough Starter

Important note: Follow directions carefully. Sourdough starters are sensitive and do not tolerate mistakes!

Total preparation time: 1 week

Step 1

1/2 cup **rye flour**

1/2 cup **warm water**

2 tablespoons **sugar**

Mix all the ingredients together in a bowl and cover with plastic wrap. Let stand 4 days at room temperature. After 4 days, check to see if the mixture has fermented. Bubbles on top indicate fermentation. If there are no bubbles, cover and let stand 1 more day.

Step 2

1/2 cup **rye flour**

1/3 cup **water**

When the mixture from Step 1 has fermented, mix in the additional rye flour and water. Cover and let stand 1 day.

Step 3

1/2 cup **bread flour**

1/4 cup **whole wheat flour**

1/4 cup **whole rye flour**

3/4 cup **water**

Check the sourdough starter. (It should have tripled in volume.) Add the flours and the water, mix well, cover with plastic wrap, and let stand 8 hours.

Step 4

31/2 cups **bread flour**

2 cups **water**

Once the mixture from Step 3 has stood for 8 hours, transfer it to the bowl of a standing electric mixture with a dough hook attached. Add the flour and water, then knead on low speed for 5 minutes. Transfer the resulting dough to a floured bowl, cover with plastic wrap, and let rest for 6 hours.

Now the sourdough starter is ready to use. If not using immediately, store in a tightly closed glass jar in the refrigerator.

To maintain sourdough starter: Always put aside about a 1/4-pound piece of any plain bread dough made with sourdough starter. The best types of bread dough to use for this purpose are Country-Style White Bread (page 90) for a regular starter, and German Sourdough Bread (page 108) for a "dark" starter, which is preferable for recipes like Real Jewish Rye (page 101). Either dough will work when making sourdough starters for sourdough breads in this book. Wrap the piece in plastic wrap and store in the refrigerator for up to 4 days, or in the freezer for up to a month.

To use stored sourdough starter: Defrost the piece of sourdough starter at room temperature and place in the bowl of a standing electric mixer. Using the dough hook, blend in 1 cup of dough and 2/3 cup water. Mix on low speed for 5 minutes. Transfer this dough to a floured bowl, cover with plastic wrap and let stand 6 hours.

After 6 hours, repeat the procedure, adding another cup of dough and 2/3 cup water. Mix on low speed for 5 minutes, place in a floured bowl, cover with plastic wrap, and let stand another 6 hours.

Now the sourdough starter is ready for use.

Discovered in Egypt more than 3,000 years ago, sourdough is one of the oldest and most primitive forms of raising bread. Created by the fermentation of starches and sugars with airborne yeast, sourdough starters and breads are the pride of professional bakers. For best results, I always measure sourdough starter by weight rather than cups.

The Baker's Techniques

Here's an outline of the basic techniques we'll be using in this book:

1

Adding Liquids and Yeast
Always add the yeast with the liquids called for in a recipe. This allows the yeast to dissolve and helps it work faster.

Adding Salt
Since salt helps regulate the yeast but will kill it if they come in direct contact, always keep the mixer running while adding salt.

The Baker's Mark
The baker's mark (*le coup de lame* in French) is the baker's "signature," slashed on his/her breads before baking. While studying in France, I learned that throughout the centuries artisan bakers have traditionally marked their loaves with special slashes to distinguish them from the work of others. But slashing serves a vital functional purpose as well: it allows breads to reach their maximum rising potential in the oven without tearing or cracking.

2

To slash a loaf before baking, use a razor-sharp blade and make quick, firm, decisive strokes. Slash the bread 1/8 inch deep. Always decide on the type of slash you wish to make before you do it. (I say this from experience!) You may choose one long slash down the center of a pan-baked loaf or several diagonal slashes on a baguette or round loaf baked directly on a pizza stone or baking sheet (see pictures 1–4).

For rolls, sharp scissors may also be used to snip the tops in a decorative fashion.

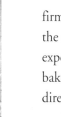

3

Glazing
Glazing (brushing a bread, yeast cake, or pastry with a substance before baking) not only effects the taste, texture, and crust of a bread but also makes the final product more attractive. Egg washes are the most common because they produce a shiny, golden-brown glaze. When a subtle olive flavor and shiny glaze is desirable, brush with olive oil instead, both before and immediately after baking.

4

Kneading

Kneading is one of the most important techniques we use in this book. It is essential for preparing dough to rise, since it distributes activated yeast throughout the dough and then helps the flour's proteins develop into gluten, which gives the dough its ability to stretch and expand. As starches are broken down to feed the yeast, bubbles of carbon dioxide gas are created and caught between the strands of gluten, causing the dough to rise. For the recipes in this book, I always use a standing electric mixer outfitted with a dough hook and knead the dough for exactly the time indicated in the recipe directions. Machine-kneading will give even first-time bakers the excellent results they might not achieve with hand-kneading.

Mixing

Always mix the ingredients together on low speed for the first 3 minutes. This blends them together in a uniform manner.

Proofing

First proofing (resting time) This is the first rising period after kneading, when the yeast begins to work. I call it "resting time" because it gives the dough its first chance to rest after its kneading workout.

Punching down

Punching down (also known as **knocking back**) After the first rising or "resting" period, it is important to punch the dough down so the next rising will be successful. To do so, remove the dough from the rising bowl and place on a floured work surface. Flatten it out with the palm of the hand to remove air pockets.

Final proofing (rising time) This is the second time the dough is allowed to rise, developing its final shape before baking. Always let the dough rise at room temperature (about 70° F to 75° F), checking its progress every 15 minutes. Do not let the dough overrise.
- If the dough rises faster than recipe directions indicate, proceed with baking. It is unnecessary to wait the full amount of time.

- If the dough does not rise as quickly as directions indicate, wait until it does.
- Bread dough should rise to at least double its initial volume, and even higher before being placed it in the oven.
- Yeast cakes should triple in volume by the end of rising time in order that the finished product be light and airy.

Ellipse

Shaping

Once the dough has gone through its first proofing (resting time), it's time to shape it. As you glance through the recipes, you'll notice that I give precise shaping instructions for each bread's desired form. While in yeast-based recipes you can feel free to experiment with a variety of imaginative shapes (including using the doughs to create rolls), for sourdough breads I recommend following the shaping directions in each recipe as closely as possible.

Loaf

Croissant

Better-Baking Tips

The Best Oven for Baking Breads

Though many people own and use convection ovens, I always recommend using a nonconvection oven for bread baking. While convection shortens baking time, bread is best when it bakes slowly, allowing the heat to penetrate throughout the loaf more evenly, the yeast or sourdough to reach its maximum height, and the bread to develop its perfect crust.

The Best Way to Bake Pastries & Cakes

Morning pastries and yeast cakes containing butter or oil fare better when baked in convection ovens with upper and lower heat sources, if possible.

Baking on a Pizza Stone or Unglazed Ceramic Tiles

For serious bread bakers, there's nothing like baking directly on a pizza stone, available all over town. Slid into the bottom of the oven, it provides a baking surface similar to that of a professional oven, with equally satisfactory results.

I recommend using a square pizza stone if possible, since it has more surface area than the round variety. If you can't find one in your local store, try ordering from an on-line supplier.

Several of my friends prefer another method: lining their ovens with unglazed ceramic tiles, leaving 2 inches of airspace from the oven walls.

Testing for Doneness

While we're usually told that color or the toothpick test is the best method to check for doneness in cake baking, in bread baking it's the knock that counts. Using oven mitts, remove the baked bread from the oven, carefully turn it over, and tap the bottom. If it emits a hollow sound, the bread is ready.

Good Morning!

Italian-Style Brioche

Just like the French love their morning croissant, so the Italians begin the day with a cup of strong espresso and a brioche. This sweet yeast dough, enriched with butter, makes a fragrant and delicious roll that's perfect for brunch as well. Although the process is time consuming, you can roll the dough into brioche shapes and freeze them for up to 2 weeks, then defrost them at room temperature and bake according to recipe directions.

1 tablespoon **dry yeast**

1/3 cup **cold milk**

3/4 cup **sugar**

4 large **eggs**

31/2 cups **bread flour** (1 pound)

1 teaspoon **dried lecithin** (optional)*

2 teaspoons **salt**

3/4 cup **butter**, room temperature

1 **egg**, beaten, for brushing

1 tablespoon **confectioners' sugar**, for garnish

Additional **flour** for assorted tasks

Preparation time: 20 minutes
Resting time: overnight
Rising time: 2 hours
Baking time: 15 minutes
Makes 10–12 brioches

1. In the bowl of a standing electric mixer with the dough hook attached, mix the yeast, milk, sugar, eggs, flour, and lecithin (if using) at low speed for 3 minutes. With the machine running, add the salt, switch to medium speed, and knead for an additional 6 minutes.

2. Switch back to low speed and gradually add the butter, kneading until a soft, uniform dough is formed.

3. Place the dough in a large floured bowl, cover with plastic wrap, and let rise overnight in the refrigerator.

4. Transfer the dough to a floured work surface and flatten it out with the palm of the hand to remove air pockets (see instructions, page 17).

5. Roll out the dough with a lightly floured rolling pin to form an 8 x 15-inch rectangle, 1/8 inch thick.

6. Use a sharp knife to cut out triangles that are 8 inches on two sides with a base of 21/2 inches. Roll each triangle from the bottom up, like a croissant (see picture, page 18).

7. Place 3 inches apart on a lightly greased or parchment paper–lined baking sheet, brush with beaten egg, and let rise 2 hours.

8. Bake in a preheated 350ºF oven for 15 minutes or until golden brown. Just before serving, sprinkle tops with confectioners' sugar.

* Lecithin powder adds texture to breads. It can be found in health food stores. Do not use roasted or liquid lecithin.

French-Style Brioche

A delicious cross between bread and cake, the butter- and egg-rich French brioche has a classic shape—a little topknot and a scalloped underside—that makes it one of the symbols of Paris. This same recipe may be prepared as individual servings (Brioche Parisienne) or as one large loaf (Brioche à Tête), or the dough may be frozen for up to 2 weeks. To use, defrost on the kitchen counter and bake according to recipe directions.

1. In the bowl of a standing electric mixer with the dough hook attached, mix the eggs, milk, yeast, sugar, and flour for 3 minutes at low speed. With the machine running, add the salt, switch to medium speed, and knead for an additional 6 minutes.

2. Switch back to low speed and gradually add the butter, kneading until a soft and uniform dough is formed.

3. Place the dough in a large floured bowl, cover the bowl tightly with plastic wrap, and let rise in the refrigerator overnight.

4. Next morning, punch down the dough (see instructions, page 17) to stop the rising process and let rest 5 minutes. Place on a lightly floured surface and divide into 3 equal balls. Cut each ball into 8 equal pieces and roll each piece into a ball. You should have a total of 24 balls.

5. Grease 24 brioche molds, each about 3½ inches in diameter and 2 inches deep, with softened butter. Place these in the refrigerator to create a hardened shell, then grease again.

6. Pinch off a small piece from each ball (about 10% of each one). Roll both the larger and smaller pieces of dough into smooth balls. Place one of the large balls in each of the prepared molds.

7. Using your forefinger, make an indentation in the center of each large ball and top each with one of the small balls, so that half the small ball is exposed.

8. Place the brioche molds on a baking tray. Brush each brioche twice with the beaten egg and let rise for 2 hours, or until the dough rises above the edges of the pan.

9. Bake in a preheated 350ºF oven for 15 minutes, or until golden brown. Let cool for 10 minutes in the molds before turning the molds over to remove the brioches. Finish cooling on a wire rack. Serve warm.

5 large **eggs**

1/4 cup **cold milk**

3 ounces **fresh yeast** or
2 tablespoons **dry yeast**

1/2 cup **sugar**

3½ cups (1 pound) **unbleached all-purpose flour**

2 teaspoons **salt**

1 cup **butter**, room temperature (plus extra for greasing molds)

1 **egg**, beaten, for brushing

Additional **flour** for assorted tasks

Special tools: **brioche molds**

Preparation time: 20 minutes
Resting time: overnight
Rising time: 2 hours
Baking time: 15 minutes
Makes 24 brioches

Italian Sweet Breakfast Rolls

These wonderful breakfast rolls are great with your morning coffee or served at the brunch table. Easy to make, they have a light texture with "dots" of sweetness thanks to the raisins. Use any leftover rolls for grilled cheese sandwiches or toast.

1. In the bowl of a standing electric mixer with the dough hook attached, mix the milk, yeast, sugar, egg, and flour on low speed for 3 minutes. With the machine running, add the salt, switch to medium speed, and knead for an additional 5 minutes. Pour in the raisins and continue to knead at medium speed for 3 minutes. Add the butter and continue kneading at medium speed for 3 minutes, or until a smooth and uniform dough is formed.

2. Cover the bowl with a kitchen towel and let rest for 1 hour.

3. Transfer the dough to a lightly floured work surface and flatten it out with the palm of the hand to remove air pockets (see "Punching down," page 17). Divide the dough into 3 equal balls and cut each ball into 6 pieces, for a total of 18 pieces. Roll each piece into a ball.

4. Line 2 baking sheets with parchment paper. Place 9 balls 2 inches apart on each sheet. Brush with beaten egg and let rise for 1 hour, or until tripled in size.

5. Preheat the oven to 350ºF and bake 15 to 20 minutes until golden brown, checking occasionally for even baking. Serve warm.

* Look for moist golden raisins for this recipe (rather than the drier types) or pour boiling water over regular raisins and let stand 1 minute. Drain well before using.

1 cup **cold milk**

1 tablespoon **dry yeast**

3/4 cup **sugar**

1 large **egg**

3½ cups **bread flour**

2 teaspoons **salt**

1½ cups **golden raisins***

1/4 cup **butter**, room temperature

1 **egg**, beaten, for brushing

Additional **flour** for assorted tasks

Preparation time: 20 minutes
Resting time: 1 hour
Rising time: 1 hour
Baking time: 15–20 minutes
Makes 18 rolls

Heavenly Apple-Cinnamon Bread

This fabulous bread is originally from the Normandy region of France, which is famous for its luscious apples. I like to bake it until it's almost done the night before and then give it a final 5 minutes in the oven just before serving. That way one can enjoy the taste, texture, and fragrance of fresh-baked bread. I recommend using fresh yeast for this bread if you can get it. It really makes a difference!

3 large **eggs**

2/3 cup **cold milk**

3 ounces **fresh yeast** or
2 tablespoons **dry yeast**

1/2 cup **sugar**

3 **Granny Smith apples**, peeled, cored, and coarsely grated

2 teaspoons **cinnamon**

4 cups **unbleached all-purpose flour**

2 teaspoons **salt**

1/2 cup **butter**, room temperature

Additional **flour** for assorted tasks

Preparation time: 20 minutes
Resting time: 1 hour
Rising time: 1 hour
Baking time: 30 minutes
Makes 2–3 oval loaves

1. In the bowl of a standing electric mixer with the dough hook attached, mix the eggs, milk, yeast, sugar, grated apples, cinnamon, and flour at low speed for 3 minutes. With the machine running, add the salt, switch to medium speed, and continue kneading for an additional 6 minutes. Switch to low speed and gradually add the butter, kneading until a uniform dough is formed.

2. Cover and let rest in a warm place for 1 hour.

3. Transfer the dough to a lightly floured work surface and flatten it out with the palm of the hand to remove air pockets (see "Punching down," page 17). Divide the dough into 2 or 3 equal pieces, knead briefly, then form each into a neat round. Let rest 5 minutes.

4. Place the palms of the hands on either side of the round and roll the dough backward and forward, keeping hands in the same position. Ease the dough into an oval shape about 10 inches long and 4 inches wide, with a rounded top and slightly tapered ends (see picture of finished bread).

5. Place the ovals on a lightly greased or parchment paper–lined baking sheet and let rise 1 hour.

6. Just before baking, use a sharp knife or single-edge razor blade to make 2 diagonal slashes in the top (see "The Baker's Mark," page 16).

7. Bake in a preheated 350ºF oven for 30 minutes or until golden brown, checking occasionally for even browning.

Luscious Peach Packages

What a special way to start the day! My favorite time to make these is in the summer, when fresh, ripe yellow peaches are really at their best, but canned peaches may be substituted if necessary. For best results, it's important to always roll the dough out while it's still chilled. Warm dough just won't give the same delicate texture.

1. In the bowl of a standing electric mixer with the dough hook attached, mix the milk, yeast, sugar, egg yolk, and flour at low speed for 3 minutes. With the machine running, add the salt, switch to medium speed, and knead for an additional 5 minutes. Gradually add the butter and continue kneading 3 minutes.

2. Cover the bowl with plastic wrap and let rest 1 hour at room temperature.

3. In the meantime, halve the peaches and cut each half into 8 thin slices. Cut each slice in half and place in a bowl. Pour the amaretto or schnapps over them, and let soak for 1 hour in the refrigerator.

4. Transfer the dough to a floured work surface and flatten it out with the palm of the hand to remove air pockets (see "Punching down," page 17). Let rest 5 minutes.

5. Divide the dough into 3 equal pieces, then each piece into 3 equal portions. You should have 9 pieces all together. Roll each into a ball.

6. On a floured work surface, using a lightly floured rolling pin, roll each ball into a 5-inch circle. Use a tablespoon to transfer about 10 pieces of the soaked peaches (with only the liquid that clings to them) to each circle. Fold the top and bottom inward over the filling like flaps, then fold the sides inward to form an envelope-like shape.

7. Grease a baking sheet or line it with parchment paper. Place the packages 1 1/2 inches apart on the baking sheet, brush them with beaten egg, and let rise for 1 hour, or until doubled in size.

8. Bake in a preheated 350ºF oven for 15 minutes, or until golden brown.

1/2 cup **cold milk**

1/2 tablespoon **dry yeast**

1/4 cup **sugar**

1 **egg yolk**

13/4 cups **bread flour**

1 teaspoon **salt**

2 tablespoons **butter**, room temperature

3 large **fresh yellow peaches**

1 tablespoon **amaretto liqueur** or **peach schnapps**

1 **egg**, beaten, for brushing

Additional **flour** for assorted tasks

Preparation time: 20 minutes
Resting time: 1 hour
Rising time: 1 hour
Baking time: 15 minutes
Makes 9 peach packages

French Country-Style Rolls

These great rolls are as appropriate for an informal breakfast as they are for a gourmet meal. Their crusty exterior and mild taste are perfect for sopping up sauces. The poolish sponge (see page 13) gives height to the loaf.

FOR THE POOLISH SPONGE:

1/2 cup **bread flour**

1/4 cup **water**

1/2 teaspoon **dry yeast**

FOR THE DOUGH:

1 1/4 cups **water**

1 tablespoon **dry yeast**

poolish sponge

3 1/2 cups **bread flour**

1 tablespoon **salt**

Additional **flour** for assorted tasks

> Preparation time for the
> poolish sponge: 1 1/2 hours
> Resting time: 1 hour
> Rising time: 1 hour
> Assembly time: 20 minutes
> Baking time: 20 minutes
> Makes 16 rolls

1. Prepare the sponge in advance by mixing the ingredients together in a small bowl, using a fork.

2. Cover with plastic wrap and let stand at room temperature for 1 1/2 hours.

3. In the bowl of a standing electric mixer with the dough hook attached, mix the water, yeast, sponge, and flour together at low speed for 3 minutes. With the machine running, add the salt, switch to medium speed, and continue to knead the mixture at for an additional 10 minutes.

4. Transfer the dough to a floured bowl, cover with plastic wrap, and let rest for 1 hour.

5. Place the dough on a floured surface and flatten it out with the palm of the hand to remove air pockets (see "Punching down," page 17). Divide the dough into 4 equal parts, then each part into 4 equal pieces. You should have a total of 16 pieces. Roll each piece into a ball and place on the floured surface. Let stand 5 minutes.

6. Place one ball on the work surface and use the palm of the hand to gently rock it back and forth until it forms an elongated shape with slightly tapered ends. Repeat the process with the remaining balls.

7. Place the elongated rolls on a floured kitchen towel and let rise 1 hour.

8. Preheat the oven to 450°F and place a square pizza stone or clean, unglazed ceramic tiles in the bottom of the oven. With a sharp knife, make a 1/8-inch-deep slash lengthwise in each roll. (For more about slashing, see "The Baker's Mark," page 16.)

9. Place 8 rolls 1/2 inch apart on the stone or tiles and bake for 10 minutes, or until a hollow sound is heard when the rolls are tapped on their underside. Remove and bake the remaining 8 rolls.

For a
Beautiful Brunch

Best Blueberry Muffins

Quick and easy, these blueberry muffins add a festive touch to any brunch. You may also use a Teflon or silicone muffin pan to make them, if desired.

1 cup **cold milk**

1/2 cup **butter**

3/4 cup fresh or frozen **blueberries**

1 1/2 cups **unbleached all-purpose flour**

1 tablespoon **baking powder**

1/2 cup **sugar**

1 teaspoon **salt**

1 large **egg**

Preparation time: 40 minutes
Baking time: 18–20 minutes
Makes about 12 muffins

1. In a small saucepan, bring the milk and butter just to a boil and remove from heat.

2. Place the blueberries in a bowl and pour the milk and butter mixture over them. Stir gently to mix.

3. Combine the dry ingredients in a separate bowl using a wooden spoon. Blend in the blueberry mixture. Add the egg and continue mixing until smooth.

4. Preheat the oven to 400°F. Grease a muffin pan (or use paper liners) and spoon the batter into the pan, filling each of the greased cups up to three-quarters full.

5. Bake for 18 to 20 minutes, or until golden and a toothpick inserted in the center of one or two of the muffins comes out clean. If necessary, turn the pan halfway through baking to ensure even browning. Carefully remove the muffins from the pan while still warm and let them finish cooling on a wire rack.

Oat-Enriched Muffins

All the goodness and health benefits of oats in one scrumptious little muffin. In my home, we serve them warm with honey butter or quality jam.

1. In a small saucepan, bring the milk and butter just to a boil and remove from heat. Pour over the oats in a bowl and mix well with a wooden spoon.

2. In another bowl, mix the dry ingredients together using a wooden spoon.

3. Add the oat mixture to the dry ingredients and mix until just blended. Add the egg and continue mixing until smooth. Do not overmix.

4. Preheat the oven to 400ºF. Grease a muffin pan (or use paper liners) and spoon the batter into the pan, filling each cup up to three-quarters full.

5. Bake for 18 to 20 minutes, or until golden and a toothpick inserted in the center of one or two muffins comes out clean. If necessary, turn the pan halfway through baking to ensure even browning. Carefully remove the muffins from the pan while still warm and let them finish cooling on a wire rack.

1 cup **cold milk**

1/2 cup **butter**

3/4 cup **quick-cooking oats**

1 cup **unbleached all-purpose flour**

1 tablespoon **baking powder**

1/2 cup **sugar**

1 teaspoon **salt**

1 large **egg**

Preparation time: 40 minutes
Baking time: 18–20 minutes
Makes 15–17 muffins

High-Fiber Bran Muffins

Get your daily quota of bran with these great muffins, perfect for brunch or a coffee break at the office.

1. In a small saucepan, bring the milk and butter just to a boil and remove from heat.

2. Put the bran in a bowl and pour the milk and butter mixture over it. Mix well with a wooden spoon.

3. Mix the dry ingredients together in a bowl. Add the bran mixture and stir until just blended. Add the egg and continue mixing until smooth.

4. Cover the bowl with plastic wrap and let stand 10 minutes.

5. Preheat the oven to 400°F. Grease a muffin pan (or use paper liners) and spoon the batter into the pan, filling each cup up to two-thirds full.

6. Bake for 18 to 20 minutes, or until golden and a toothpick inserted in the center of one or two of the muffins comes out clean. If necessary, turn the pan halfway through baking to ensure even browning. Carefully remove the muffins from the pan while still warm and let them finish cooling on a wire rack.

1 cup **cold milk**

1/2 cup **butter**

3/4 cup **wheat bran**

3/4 cup **unbleached all-purpose flour**

1/3 cup **whole rye flour**

1/3 cup **whole wheat flour**

1 tablespoon **baking powder**

1/2 cup **sugar**

1 teaspoon **salt**

1 large **egg**

Preparation time: 40 minutes
Baking time: 18–20 minutes
Makes about 15 muffins

Rich Yeast Pastry
With Vanilla Pastry Cream Filling

This is one of my favorite all-purpose pastries. Like Danish pastry, you can form it into all kinds of shapes, like round, knotted, or twisted rolls, and fill with Vanilla Pastry Cream (recipe follows), Chocolate Pastry Cream (see recipe for Chocolate Brioche, page 44), or even cream cheese or nuts. For best results, I recommend using fresh yeast for this pastry.

2/3 cup **cold milk**

2 1/4 ounces **fresh yeast** or 1 1/2 tablespoons **dry yeast**

1 large **egg**

2/3 cup **sugar**

1/4 teaspoon freshly grated **lemon rind**

1/4 teaspoon **vanilla** (optional)

3 1/2 cups **unbleached all-purpose flour**

1/4 teaspoon **salt**

1/3 cup **butter**, room temperature

Vanilla Pastry Cream Filling (recipe follows)

1/2 cup **dark raisins**, soaked in 2 tablespoons **rum** for 1 hour or more

1 **egg**, beaten, for brushing

Additional **flour** for assorted tasks

Preparation time: 1 1/2 hours
Resting time: 1 hour
Rising time: 1 1/2–2 hours
Baking time: about 15 minutes
Makes 12–14 pastries

1. In the bowl of a standing electric mixer with the dough hook attached, mix the milk, yeast, egg, sugar, lemon rind, vanilla (if using), and flour at low speed for 3 minutes. With the machine running, add the salt, switch to medium speed, and continue to knead at for an additional 7 minutes. Gradually add the butter and knead 3 minutes.

2. Cover with plastic wrap and let rest 1 hour.

3. Transfer the dough to a floured work surface and flatten it out with the palm of the hand to remove air pockets (see "Punching down," page 17). At this point the dough may be wrapped in plastic wrap and frozen, if desired. Defrost at room temperature for 3 hours before using.

4. Prepare the Vanilla Pastry Cream Filling as directed in the recipe on page 43.

5. Using a lightly floured rolling pin, roll out the dough on a floured board to form a 15 x 15-inch square and spread the vanilla pastry cream uniformly on top with an offset spatula.

6. Sprinkle the raisins on top of the pastry cream and roll up like a jelly roll.

7. Cut the roll into 1/2-inch-thick slices with a sharp (nonserrated) knife and place flat side down on a parchment paper–lined baking sheet, leaving 2 inches between each slice.

8. Brush each slice with the beaten egg and let rise for 1 1/2 to 2 hours, until tripled in size. Bake in a preheated 350ºF oven for 15 minutes, or until golden brown and shiny.

NOTE: The Vanilla Pastry Cream Filling can be prepared up to 48 hours in advance and should be well chilled before using.

Vanilla Pastry Cream Filling

1. In a small saucepan, bring the milk and half the sugar just to a boil and remove from heat. Stir in the vanilla.

2. Whisk the egg yolks, remaining sugar, and cornstarch together in a separate bowl using a wire whisk.

3. Quickly whisk 1/3 of the boiled milk into the egg mixture and beat constantly to blend. Pour the egg mixture into the saucepan, whisking constantly.

4. Heat the mixture over low heat and continue stirring just until the cream is thick and lightly bubbling.

5. Remove from heat, cover, and chill in the refrigerator until ready to use.

2 cups **cold milk**

1 cup **sugar**

1 teaspoon **vanilla**

7 **egg yolks**

3 tablespoons **cornstarch**

Chocolate Brioche

A winning combination of delicate brioche dough and rich chocolate filling. Bet you can't eat just one! Since the brioche dough must be chilled overnight, I also like to prepare the filling the night before to let the chocolate balls sit in the refrigerator along with the dough. That way everything is ready to go when I wake up in the morning.

5 large **eggs**

1/4 cup **cold milk**

11/2 ounces **fresh yeast** or
1 tablespoon **dry yeast**

1/2 cup **sugar**

31/2 cups **unbleached all-purpose flour**

2 teaspoons **salt**

1 cup **butter**, room temperature

1 **egg**, beaten, for brushing

Chocolate Pastry Cream (recipe follows)

Additional **flour** for assorted tasks

Special tools: **brioche molds**

Preparation time: 40 minutes
Resting time: overnight
Rising time: 2 hours
Baking time: 12–13 minutes
Makes 12 brioches

1. In the bowl of a standing electric mixer with the dough hook attached, mix the eggs, milk, yeast, sugar, and flour at low speed for 3 minutes. With the machine running, add the salt, switch to medium speed, and continue to knead for an additional 7 minutes. Gradually add the butter and knead 3 minutes until a smooth, uniform dough is formed.

2. Cover with plastic wrap and let rest overnight in the refrigerator.

3. Grease hands with a little oil. Remove 1 heaping teaspoon of the chocolate mixture and roll between the palms of the hands to form a 1-inch ball. Place on a plate lined with waxed paper. Repeat with the remaining chocolate mixture. Keep refrigerated until ready to use.

4. Transfer the dough to a floured work surface and flatten it out with the palm of the hand to remove air pockets (see "Punching down," page 17). Divide the dough into 3 equal pieces, then each one of the pieces into 4. Roll each into a neat ball for a total of 12 balls.

5. Using your forefinger, make an indentation in each ball of dough and gently press in a chilled chocolate ball, so that the top of the chocolate ball is level with the dough. Place each ball in a twice-greased (see step 4, page 25) small brioche mold. Place the brioche molds 1 inch apart on a baking sheet and brush with beaten egg.

6. Let rise for 2 hours, or until tripled in size.

7. Bake in a preheated 350ºF oven 12 to 13 minutes or until golden brown.

NOTE: It is imperative to work with chilled dough throughout the shaping process. Since your hands tend to heat the dough as you handle it, you may want to wrap it in plastic wrap and place it in the freezer for a few minutes until firm.

Chocolate Pastry Cream

1. Break the chocolate into pieces and place in a bowl.

2. Bring the cream to a boil in a small saucepan and pour over the chocolate. Mix with a wire whisk until smooth.

3. Stir in the liqueur.

4. Chill at least 4 hours in the refrigerator.

7½ ounces good-quality **bittersweet chocolate** (at least 50% cocoa solids)

¾ cup **sweet cream**

1 tablespoon **coffee liqueur or another liqueur of your choice**

Florida Citrus Brioche

The fragrant citrus scent of these brioches make them irresistible.

5 large **eggs**

1/4 cup **cold milk**

3 ounces **fresh yeast** or
2 tablespoons **dry yeast**

1/2 cup **sugar**

2 teaspoons **citrus or orange extract**

2 teaspoons grated **orange rind**

2 tablespoons high-quality **orange liqueur** (like **Cointreau** or **Grand Marnier**)

3 1/2 cups **unbleached all-purpose flour**

2 teaspoons **salt**

1 cup **butter**, room temperature

1 **egg**, beaten, for brushing

12 thin **orange** half-slices, with peel, for garnish

Additional **flour** for assorted tasks

Preparation time: 20 minutes.
Resting time: overnight
Rising time: 2 hours
Baking time: 15 minutes
Makes 12 brioches

1. In the bowl of a standing electric mixture with the dough hook attached, mix the eggs, milk, yeast, sugar, extract, grated orange rind, orange liqueur, and flour for 3 minutes at low speed. With the machine running, switch to medium speed, add the salt, and knead for 7 minutes. Gradually add the butter and continue kneading 3 minutes, until a smooth, uniform dough is formed.

2. Cover with plastic wrap and let rest overnight in the refrigerator.

3. Transfer the dough to a floured work surface and flatten it out with the palm of the hand to remove air pockets (see "Punching down," page 17). Divide the dough into 3 equal parts, then each part into 4 pieces, for a total of 12.

4. Roll each piece into a ball and place each ball in an aluminum foil muffin cup. Brush with beaten egg and top with a twisted half-slice of orange. Let rise at room temperature for 2 hours, or until tripled in size.

5. Bake in a preheated 350ºF oven for 15 minutes, or until golden brown.

Rye & Raisin Rolls

These classic rolls are originally from the Swiss-German border, where they are often served with aged meats or cheeses. The combination of rye flour and raisins gives them their special flavor.

1 cup **water**

1 ounce **fresh yeast** or
2 teaspoons **dry yeast**

¼ pound **fermented dough** (see page 12)

¼ pound small **dark raisins**

2 cups **bread flour**

¾ cup **whole rye flour**

2 teaspoons **salt**

Additional **flour** for assorted tasks

> **Preparation time: 20 minutes**
> **Resting time: 1 hour**
> **Rising time: 1 hour and 15 minutes**
> **Baking time: 30 minutes**
> **Makes 8 rolls**

1. In the bowl of a standing electric mixer with the dough hook attached, mix the water, yeast, fermented dough, raisins, bread flour, and rye flour at low speed for 3 minutes. With the machine running, add the salt and continue kneading at medium speed for 12 minutes.

2. Place the dough in a floured bowl, cover with plastic wrap, and let rest for 1 hour at room temperature.

3. Transfer the dough to a floured work surface and flatten it out with the palm of the hand to remove air pockets (see "Punching down," page 17). Divide the dough into 2 equal parts, then each part into 4 pieces, for a total of 8.

4. Roll each piece into a neat ball and place 1 inch apart on a parchment paper–lined baking sheet.

5. Let rise for 1 hour and 15 minutes, or until doubled in size.

6. Use a pair of sharp scissors to make ½-inch-deep snips in the tops, forming little peaks (see picture).

7.   Bake in a preheated 420ºF oven for 30 minutes, or until dark brown (the rye flour gives the rolls their distinctive color) and a knock on the bottom of the rolls produces a hollow sound.

Chocolate Chip Rolls

Children of all ages will love these chocolate chip rolls, a delicious change from chocolate chip cookies or muffins. May be baked almost completely and frozen. To use, remove from the freezer and defrost at room temperature, then bake 3 to 4 minutes and serve warm.

1. In the bowl of a standing electric mixer with the dough hook attached, mix the milk, yeast, sugar, egg, flour, and chocolate chips at low speed for 3 minutes. With the machine running, add the salt, switch to medium speed, and knead for an additional 7 minutes. Gradually add the butter and continue kneading 3 minutes, until a smooth, uniform dough is formed.

2. Place the dough in a floured bowl, cover with plastic wrap, and let rest for 1 hour.

3. Transfer the dough to a floured work surface and flatten it out with the palm of the hand to remove air pockets (see "Punching down," page 17). Divide the dough into 3 equal parts, then each part into 4 pieces, for a total of 12.

4. Roll each piece into a neat ball and place 2 inches apart on a parchment paper–lined baking sheet.

5. Let rise for 1 hour, or until doubled in size.

6. Preheat the oven to 375ºF. Brush the balls with beaten egg and bake for 15 minutes, or until golden brown.

1 cup **cold milk**

3 ounces **fresh yeast** or
2 tablespoons **dry yeast**

1/2 cup **sugar**

1 large **egg**

3 1/2 cups **bread flour**

1 cup **chocolate chips**

2 teaspoons **salt**

1/4 cup **butter**, room temperature

1 **egg**, beaten, for brushing

Additional **flour** for assorted tasks

Preparation time: 20 minutes
Resting time: 1 hour
Rising time: 1 hour
Baking time: 15 minutes
Makes 12 rolls

Delicate Butter Bread

This tasty bread is not only great for brunch but also makes great sandwiches (my favorite is smoked salmon) and toast. Uniquely shaped, the loaves can be easily "torn" into individual rolls.

1 cup **water**

2 ounces **fresh yeast** or
4 teaspoons **dry yeast**

1/3 cup **butter**, room temperature

11/4 pounds **fermented dough**
(see page 12)

3 cups **bread flour**

2 teaspoons **salt**

1 **egg**, beaten with 2 tablespoons
cold **milk**, for brushing

Additional **flour** for assorted
tasks

Preparation time: 20 minutes
Resting time: 1 hour
Rising time: 1 hour
Baking time: 35–40 minutes
Makes 2 loaves

1. In the bowl of a standing electric mixer with the dough hook attached, mix the water, yeast, butter, fermented dough, and flour at low speed for 3 minutes. While the machine is running, add the salt, switch to medium speed, and continue to knead for 10 minutes, or until smooth.

2. Cover the bowl with a kitchen towel and let rest for 1 hour.

3. Transfer the dough to a floured surface and divide the dough into 2 equal parts, then each part into 5 pieces, for a total of 10. Roll each piece into a ball.

4. To achieve the special shape of these loaves, place 5 balls together in a straight line (like a caterpillar) and press to "fasten." Repeat with the remaining 5 balls. You will have two loaves.

5. Place the loaves on a parchment paper–lined (or greased) baking sheet and brush with the beaten egg mixture. Let rise for 1 hour, or until doubled in size.

6. Bake in a preheated 400ºF oven for 35 to 40 minutes, until the loaves are brandy colored.

Walnut & Prune Bread

This recipe comes from southwestern France, known for its luscious summer plums that are dried to make prunes for the winter months. For best results, advance preparation of any of the steps is not recommended. While this bread can be baked in a baking pan, I recommend baking it on a pizza stone or oven tiles for best results. The bread stays fresh for up to 3 days.

1 cup **water**

2 tablespoons **dry yeast**

¼ pound **fermented dough** (see page 12)

¼ pound **walnuts**

¼ pound **whole pitted prunes**

2 cups **bread flour**

¾ cup **whole rye flour**

2 teaspoons **salt**

Additional **flour** for assorted tasks

Preparation time: 20 minutes
Resting time: 1 hour
Rising time: 1 hour
Baking time: 40 minutes
Makes 2 loaves

---

1. In the bowl of a standing electric mixer with the dough hook attached, mix the water, yeast, fermented dough, walnuts, prunes, bread flour, and rye flour at low speed for 3 minutes. With the machine running, switch to medium speed, add the salt, and continue kneading for 12 minutes.

2. Place the dough in a floured bowl and cover with a kitchen towel. Let rest 1 hour.

3. Transfer the dough to a floured surface and flatten it out with the palm of the hand to remove air pockets (see "Punching down," page 17). Divide the dough into 2 equal parts.

4. Shape each piece into a round. Place the palms of the hands on either side of one round and gently roll the dough side to side while keeping hands in the same position. Continue to roll until the dough is about 10 inches long. Repeat with the other round.

5. Place each loaf on a floured kitchen towel and let rise for 1 hour.

6. Turn the loaves over and make 2 diagonal slashes on top. (On making slashes, see "The Baker's Mark," page 16.)

7. Place a square pizza stone or unglazed ceramic tiles on the bottom of the oven and preheat to 450ºF. Place the loaves 2 inches apart on the stone or tiles and bake for 40 minutes, or until dark brown and a knock on the bottom of the loaves produces a hollow sound.

NOTE: Do not use a convection oven for this recipe.

Tea for Two (or More)

English Tea-Sandwich Bread

This is the bread used to make those famous little sandwiches, buttered and stuffed with thinly sliced cucumbers, cheeses, or ham, and served along with scones at High Tea throughout the British Isles. We also enjoy it with butter and jam at breakfast and to make super grilled-cheese sandwiches.

1. In the bowl of a standing electric mixer with the dough hook attached, mix the water, milk, sugar, yeast, egg yolk, butter, and flour at low speed for 3 minutes. With the machine running, add the salt and continue to knead at low speed for 12 minutes.

2. Transfer the dough to a floured bowl, cover with plastic wrap, and let rest for 2 hours.

3. Place the dough on a floured work surface and flatten it out with the palm of the hand to remove air pockets (see "Punching down," page 17).

4. Form a ball of dough and place the palms of the hands on top of it. Roll the dough backward and forward, keeping hands in the same position, easing the ball into an oval shape about 12 inches long.

5. Place in a greased 12-inch loaf pan, brush with the beaten egg, and let rise 1 hour, or until the dough rises above the edges of the pan.

6. Bake in a preheated 400°F oven for 45 minutes, or until deep brown and shiny.

7. Let cool in the pan for 10 minutes, then remove from the pan to finish cooling on a wire rack for at least 1 hour before serving.

NOTE: This bread can be fully baked and frozen.

1 cup **water**

1/4 cup **cold milk**

3 tablespoons **sugar**

1 tablespoon **dry yeast**

1 **egg yolk**

1/4 cup **butter**, room temperature

3 1/2 cups **bread flour**

2 teaspoons **salt**

1 **egg**, beaten, for brushing

Additional **flour** for assorted tasks

Preparation time: 20 minutes
Resting time: 2 hours
Rising time: 1 hour
Baking time: 45 minutes
Makes one 12-inch loaf
(14–15 slices)

Amaretto Almond Rolls

I first had this double-almond experience (almonds and Italian amaretto liqueur) served alongside a cup of piping hot espresso in a little café in Florence, Italy.
If you'd like, prepare the dough in advance and freeze it, then let it defrost on the kitchen counter and rise until more than doubled in size before proceeding with Step 3.

1 cup **cold milk**

3 ounces **fresh yeast** or
2 tablespoons **dry yeast**

1/3 cup **sugar**

1 large **egg**

2 1/2 cups **bread flour**

1 cup ground **blanched almonds**

3 tablespoons real **amaretto liqueur**

1 teaspoon **salt**

1/4 cup **butter**, room temperature

1 egg, beaten, for brushing

brown sugar and **sliced almonds,** for garnish

Additional **flour** for assorted tasks

Preparation time: 20 minutes
Resting time: 1 hour
Rising time: 1 hour
Baking time: 15 minutes
Makes 10 rolls

1. In the bowl of a standing electric mixer with the dough hook attached, mix the milk, yeast, sugar, egg, flour, almonds, and liqueur at low speed for 3 minutes. With the mixer running, add the salt, switch to medium speed, and continue kneading for 7 minutes. Gradually add the butter and knead an additional 3 minutes until a smooth, uniform dough is formed.

2. Cover with plastic wrap and let rest 1 hour.

3. Transfer the dough to a floured work surface and flatten it out with the palm of the hand to remove air pockets (see "Punching down," page 17). Divide the dough into 2 equal parts, then each part into 5 pieces, for a total of 10.

4. Shape one piece at a time into a round roll. Holding hands at a 45-degree angle to the roll, use the outer edge of the palms to gently roll the dough backward and forward. Continue to roll until the dough is about 4 to 5 inches long and rounded in the center, with tapered edges (see picture). Repeat with the remaining pieces.

5. Place the rolls 2 inches apart on a parchment paper–lined baking sheet and brush with the beaten egg. Sprinkle a little brown sugar and a few almonds on top and let rise for 1 hour.

6. Bake in a preheated 400ºF oven for 15 minutes, or until golden brown.

Alsatian Kugelhof

This rich yeast cake hails from the Alsace region of France, where it is always served with premium tea or coffee. Prepare 1 day in advance if desired, cover with a kitchen towel, and store in a dry place. Use within 2 to 3 days.

1. Prepare the sponge in advance by mixing the water, flour, and dry yeast in a small bowl using a fork. Cover with plastic wrap and let stand at room temperature for 8 hours.

2. In a small bowl, soak the raisins in the rum for 1 hour.

3. In the bowl of a standing electric mixer with the dough hook attached, mix the fresh yeast, milk, sugar, egg yolks, sponge dough, and flour for 3 minutes at low speed. With the machine running, add the salt and knead for 7 minutes. Gradually add the butter and continue kneading for an additional 2 minutes, until a soft and uniform dough is formed.

4. Pour in the raisins with their liquid and mix for 2 more minutes.

5. Transfer the dough to a floured bowl and cover with plastic wrap. Let rest 6 hours in the refrigerator.

6. Place the dough on a floured work surface and flatten it out with the palm of the hand to remove air pockets (see "Punching down," page 17). Roll the dough into a ball and set aside for 5 minutes.

7. Use your hands to form a 15-inch-long cylinder, overlap the edges to form a circle, and gently roll them together on a floured surface. Garnish with almonds.

8. Place the ring in a well-greased 9-inch (10-cup) kugelhof pan and let rise for 1½ hours.

9. Bake in a preheated 350°F oven for 35 minutes, or until a toothpick inserted in the cake comes out clean. Let cool slightly before removing from the pan. Finish cooling on a wire rack.

FOR THE SPONGE DOUGH:

½ cup **water**

1 cup **flour**

1 teaspoon **dry yeast**

FOR THE DOUGH:

1 cup **raisins**

2 tablespoons **rum**

2 ounces **fresh yeast** or 4 teaspoons **dry yeast**

⅓ cup **cold milk**

½ cup **sugar**

3 **egg yolks**

sponge dough

2½ cups **unbleached all-purpose flour**

1 teaspoon **salt**

½ cup **butter**, room temperature

sliced almonds, for garnish

Additional **flour** for assorted tasks

Time to prepare the sponge
dough: 8 hours
Preparation time: 20 minutes
Resting time: 6 hours
Rising time: 1½ hours
Baking time: 35 minutes
Makes a 9-inch cake
(12–14 servings)

Two-Way Babka

I use this basic babka dough (a lower-fat version of brioche) together with Russian Chocolate Filling (page 66) to create two very different chocolate experiences: Chocolate-Filled Babka, a classic that Seinfeld would undoubtedly love, and Chocolate Rose Cake, an easy-to-make cake with a spectacular presentation.

FOR THE SPONGE DOUGH:

1/2 cup **water**

1 cup **flour**

1 teaspoon **dry yeast** or 1/2 ounce **fresh yeast**

FOR THE DOUGH:

1/2 cup **cold milk**

3 ounces **fresh yeast** or 2 tablespoons **dry yeast**

1/2 cup **sugar**

3 **egg yolks**

sponge dough

21/2 cups **unbleached all-purpose flour**

1 teaspoon **salt**

1/2 cup **butter**, room temperature

1. Prepare the sponge dough in advance by mixing the water, flour, and yeast together in a small bowl, using a fork. Cover with plastic wrap and let stand at room temperature for 8 hours.

2. In the bowl of a standing electric mixer with the dough hook attached, combine the milk, yeast, sugar, egg yolks, sponge dough, and flour and mix at low speed for 3 minutes. While the machine is running, add the salt, switch to medium speed, and knead for 7 minutes. Add the butter and continue kneading until a smooth dough is formed.

3. Transfer the dough to an oiled bowl, cover with plastic wrap, and let rest 6 hours in the refrigerator.

4. Place the dough on a floured work surface and flatten it out with the palm of the hand to remove air pockets (see "Punching down," page 17).

5. Divide the dough in half and follow the instructions for either Chocolate-Filled Babka or Chocolate Rose Cake, or wrap the dough in plastic wrap and freeze for up to two weeks. Defrost at room temperature before proceeding.

Tip: Don't skimp on rising time in this recipe. For best results, use no shortcuts!

> **Preparation of the sponge dough: 8 hours**
> **Preparation of the dough: 40 minutes**
> **Resting time: 6 hours or overnight**
> **Baking time: 35 minutes**
> **Makes 2 Chocolate-Filled Babkas or Chocolate Rose Cakes**
> **(or 1 of each)**

Chocolate Rose Cake

To make a sensational Chocolate Rose Cake, all you need is half the dough from the Two-Way Babka recipe (opposite) and the Russian Chocolate Filling (page 66).

FOR EACH ROSE CAKE:

1/2 **Two-Way Babka recipe**
(1 piece of divided dough)

Russian Chocolate Filling
(page 66)

1 **egg**, beaten, for brushing

Additional **flour** for assorted tasks

Special tools: **10-cup round mold with tube in center**

Rising time: 1 1/2 hours
Baking time: 35 minutes
Makes 1 cake (10–12 servings)

1. On a floured work surface, divide the dough into 2 equal pieces. Using a floured rolling pin, roll each piece into an 8 x 12-inch rectangle, 1/8 inch thick. Spread half the filling on each and roll up firmly from the long side, like you would a jelly roll. Using a sharp knife dipped in water, cut the roll into 2-inch-wide slices.

2. Thoroughly grease a 10-cup round mold with a tube in the center and arrange the slices cut side up (with the filling exposed), slightly overlapping. Brush with the beaten egg and let rise 1 1/2 hours, or until tripled in size.

3. Bake in a preheated 350ºF oven for 35 minutes, or until browned. Let cool for 1 hour in the pan, then transfer to a wire rack to finish cooling.

Chocolate-Filled Babka

To make a sensational Chocolate-Filled Babka, all you need is half the dough from the Two-Way Babka recipe (page 64), and the Russian Chocolate Filling (below).

FOR EACH BABKA:

1/2 **Two-Way Babka recipe**
(1 piece of divided dough)

Russian Chocolate Filling
(recipe follows)

1 **egg**, beaten, for brushing

Additional **flour** for assorted tasks

Special tools: **loaf pan** or **round**

Rising time: 1 1/2 hours
Baking time: 30 minutes
Makes 1 babka (10–12 servings)

1. On a floured work surface, divide the dough into 2 equal pieces. Using a floured rolling pin, roll each into a 4 x 10-inch rectangle, 1/8 inch thick. Spread half the filling on each and roll up firmly from the long side, like you would a jelly roll. Twist the two pieces together and pinch the ends closed.

2. Place the twist in a greased 10-inch loaf pan (I like to use a disposable aluminum pan for easy clean-up) or a well-greased round 10-cup mold with a center tube.

3. Brush with the beaten egg and let rise for 1 1/2 hours, or until tripled in size.

4. Bake in a preheated 350ºF oven for 30 minutes, or until browned. Let cool in the pan for 1 hour, remove from the pan to finish cooling on a wire rack before serving.

Russian Chocolate Filling

One of my fondest childhood memories is of my grandmother's Russian Chocolate Coffee Cake, made with this delicious chocolate filling.

6 ounces **bittersweet chocolate**

1/3 cup good-quality **cocoa**

1/3 cup **butter**, room temperature

1/2 cup **sugar**

1. Break the chocolate into pieces and place in the bowl of a food processor. Process until the chocolate is crushed into small pieces.

2. Combine with the remaining ingredients in a medium bowl, using a wooden spoon.

Makes enough for 1 Babka or 1 Rose Cake (10–12 servings)

Superb

Sandwich Breads

Mushroom-Shaped Sandwich Rolls

In my house these crusty rolls are particularly popular with the kids. I like to bake them until almost done, cool, and then wrap them individually in plastic wrap. They'll stay good in the freezer for up to 2 weeks. Whenever I need a few, I defrost them at room temperature and bake them 3 to 4 minutes in a preheated 450°F oven until golden brown.

1⅓ cups **water**

1 tablespoon **dry yeast**

2 teaspoons **non-fat dry milk**

3½ cups **bread flour**

2 teaspoons **salt**

½ cup **wheat germ**, for garnish

water, for dabbing

Additional **flour** for assorted tasks

Preparation time: 20 minutes
Resting time: 1½ hours
Rising time: 1 hour
Baking time: 15 minutes
Makes 6 rolls

1. In the bowl of a standing electric mixer with the dough hook attached, mix the water, yeast, milk powder, and flour at low speed for 3 minutes. With the machine running, add the salt and continue kneading at low speed for 7 minutes.

2. Place the dough in a floured bowl and let rest for 1½ hours.

3. Transfer the dough to a floured work surface and flatten with the palm of the hand to remove air pockets (see "Punching down," page 17).

4. Divide the dough in half, then each half into 4 equal pieces. Roll 2 pieces together into a ball and set aside on the work surface. Now roll each of the remaining 6 pieces into separate balls and set aside.

5. Using a lightly floured rolling pin, roll out the large ball (made of 2 pieces) to a thickness of ⅛ inch and sprinkle half the wheat germ on top. Roll over it again to fasten the wheat germ to the dough, turn over, and repeat the process with the rest of the wheat germ.

6. Use a 4-inch cookie cutter or the bottom of a round plate to cut out 6 circles. Place the circles on a floured kitchen towel. Use a finger to moisten the center of each circle with a little water and stick one of the balls on top. Let rise for 1 hour.

7. Place a square pizza stone or unglazed ceramic tiles in the bottom of the oven and preheat to 450°F.

8. Turn the rolls over so that the circle is on top and place them directly on the pizza stone. Bake for 15 minutes, or until golden brown and a knock on the bottom produces a hollow sound. Remove from the oven, let cool fully on a wire rack, and freeze individually in plastic wrap, if desired.

French Ciabatta

Although most people consider ciabatta bread an Italian specialty, the French have their own version with a more tender crumb due to the addition of olive oil. The key to success with ciabatta is more kneading than that required by most breads in order to get a soft, delicate, aerated texture. Like the Mushroom-Shaped Sandwich Rolls, ciabatta sandwich rolls can be baked until almost done, cooled, wrapped tightly in plastic wrap, and frozen for up to 2 weeks.
To use, defrost at room temperature and bake 3 to 4 minutes until golden brown.

1¼ cups **water**

1 tablespoon **dry yeast**

¼ cup **extra-virgin olive oil**

3½ cups **bread flour**

2 teaspoons **salt**

Additional **flour** for assorted tasks

Preparation time: 30 minutes
Resting time: 40 minutes
Rising time: 50 minutes
Baking time: 15 minutes
Makes 8 rolls

---

1. In the bowl of a standing electric mixer with the dough hook attached, mix the water, yeast, olive oil, and flour at low speed for 3 minutes. With the machine running, add the salt, switch to medium speed, and continue kneading for an additional 22 minutes.

2. Place the dough in a large floured bowl and cover with plastic wrap. Let rest for 40 minutes.

3. Transfer the dough to a floured work surface and flatten it out with the palm of the hand to remove air pockets (see "Punching down," page 17).

4. Using a lightly floured rolling pin, roll the dough into a 12 x 10-inch rectangle, ½ inch thick.

5. Carefully transfer the dough to a floured kitchen towel, cover with another kitchen towel, and let rise for 50 minutes.

6. Place a square pizza stone or unglazed ceramic tiles in the oven and preheat to 420ºF.

7. Using a sharp knife or single-edge razor blade, cut the dough (still on the towel) into 8 rectangles, each 6 x 2½ inches. Working quickly, turn each one over on a wooden pizza paddle and place with the puffed side down directly on the pizza stone or tiles, one finger's width apart. (They rise, rather than spread.) Bake for 15 minutes, or until browned on top and a knock on the bottom produces a hollow sound.

Everybody Loves Hamburger Rolls

Once you taste these fresh-baked, fragrant hamburger rolls, you'll wonder how you ever ate the commercial kind. Since they're so easy to make, I often bake them with my children. In fact, I usually make double the amount, wrap half the unbaked dough circles individually, and freeze them for future use. When I want to use them, I simply place the frozen circles in a parchment paper–lined baking pan and let them defrost at room temperature. Then I brush them with egg, sprinkle sesame seeds on top, and let them rise until tripled in size before I bake them. If there are any leftovers (which is seldom), I freeze baked rolls for up to 2 weeks.

1 cup **water**

1 tablespoon **dry yeast**

1 tablespoon **non-fat dry milk**

2 tablespoons **sugar**

1/4 cup **butter**, room temperature

31/4 cups **bread flour**

2 teaspoons **salt**

1 **egg**, beaten, for brushing

2 tablespoons **sesame seeds**, for garnish

Additional **flour** for assorted tasks

Preparation time: 20 minutes
Resting time: 1 hour
Rising time: 1 hour
Baking time: 15 minutes
Makes 8 rolls

1. In the bowl of a standing electric mixer with the dough hook attached, mix the water, yeast, milk powder, sugar, butter, and flour at low speed for 5 minutes. With the machine running, add the salt, switch to medium speed, and continue kneading for 10 minutes. Stop occasionally to wipe down the sides of the bowl with a rubber spatula, if necessary.

2. Place the dough in a large floured bowl and cover with plastic wrap. Let rest for 1 hour.

3. Transfer the dough to a floured work surface and flatten it out with the palm of the hand to remove air pockets (see "Punching down," page 17).

4. Divide the dough in half, then each half into 4 equal pieces, for a total of 8. Form each piece into a ball.

5. Using a lightly floured rolling pin, roll each ball into a 1/2-inch-thick circle. Place the dough circles in a parchment paper–lined baking pan 1 inch apart, brush with beaten egg, and sprinkle sesame seeds on top. Let rise for 1 hour.

6. Bake in a preheated 350ºF oven for 15 minutes, or until golden brown.

Dairy Farm Fresh Rolls

For the ultimate experience, serve these lovely rolls (called petit pain au lait *in French) freshly baked and stuffed with salmon, prosciutto, mortadella or mozzarella, and roasted vegetables.*

1. In the bowl of a standing electric mixer with the dough hook attached, mix the milk, sugar, yeast, butter, and flour at low speed for 3 minutes. With the machine running, add the salt and continue to knead at low speed for 7 minutes. Increase the mixer speed to medium and knead an additional 5 minutes.

2. Place the dough in a large floured bowl, cover with plastic wrap, and let rest for 1 hour.

3. Transfer the dough to a floured work surface and flatten it out with the palm of the hand to remove air pockets (see "punching down," page 17).

4. Divide the dough into 3 equal parts, then each part into 2 pieces, for a total of 6. Form each piece into a neat ball. Let rest 5 minutes.

5. Taking 1 ball at a time, use the palms of the hands to roll the dough backward and forward, keeping hands in the same position. Ease it into an oval shape about 10 inches long with a slightly rounded top and slightly tapered ends. Place on a parchment paper–lined baking sheet, brush with the beaten egg and milk mixture, and let rise 1 hour.

6. Bake in a preheated 350ºF oven for 15 minutes, or until browned and shiny.

11/4 cups **cold milk**

2 tablespoons **sugar**

1 tablespoon **dry yeast**

1/4 cup **butter**, room temperature

31/2 cups **bread flour**

2 teaspoons **salt**

1 **egg**, beaten with 2 tablespoons **milk**, for brushing

Additional **flour** for assorted tasks

Preparation time: 20 minutes
Resting time: 1 hour
Rising time: 1 hour
Baking time: 15 minutes
Makes 6 rolls

Mediterranean Pita Bread

In many Mediterranean countries pita bread is a staff of life. Stuffed with falafel or dipped into savory hummus, it's hard to imagine a day without it. Best served warm.

1¼ cups **water**

1 tablespoon **dry yeast**

2 tablespoons **sugar**

3½ cups **unbleached all-purpose flour**

2 teaspoons **salt**

Additional **flour** for assorted tasks

Preparation time: 20 minutes
Resting time: 1 hour
Rising time: 30 minutes
Baking time: 5 minutes
Makes 10 pitas

1. In the bowl of a standing electric mixer with the dough hook attached, mix the water, yeast, sugar, and flour at low speed for 5 minutes. With the machine running, add the salt, switch to medium speed, and continue kneading for 10 minutes.

2. Place the dough in a floured bowl and cover with plastic wrap. Let rest for 1 hour.

3. Transfer the dough to a floured work surface and flatten it out with the palm of the hand to remove air pockets (see "Punching down," page 17). Divide the dough into 10 equal pieces and roll each piece into a ball. Let rise on a floured surface for 30 minutes.

4. In the meantime, place a square pizza stone or unglazed ceramic tiles in the bottom of the oven and preheat to 450°F.

5. Using a rolling pin, roll each ball into a 5- to 6-inch circle, ⅛ inch thick. Using a pizza paddle, place the pitas on the pizza stone or ceramic tiles (in 2 batches if necessary) and bake for 5 minutes, or until puffed with light brown spots on top.

6. Remove from oven and let cool on a wire rack.

NOTES: Since the baking time is quite short, I recommend remaining close to the oven so the pitas can be removed as soon as they're done.

Pita may be frozen for up to 2 weeks. Defrost at room temperature. Reheat briefly in a hot oven, if desired.

Country-Style Ciabatta Bread

I love these little breads (called ciabatta con latte *in Italian) because of their thick, crispy exterior and light, textured interior. They may be partially baked until lightly browned, then frozen for up to 2 weeks. To use, defrost at room temperature and finish baking in a preheated 450°F oven 3 to 4 minutes.*

FOR THE SPONGE DOUGH:

1/2 cup **water**

1 cup **flour**

1/2 tablespoon **dry yeast**

FOR THE DOUGH:

1/2 cup **water**

1 cup **dry yeast**

sponge dough

3/4 cup **cold milk**

31/2 cups **bread flour**

1 tablespoon **salt**

Additional **flour** for assorted tasks.

Preparation time for the sponge dough: 2 hours
Preparation time for the dough: 20 minutes
Resting time: 40 minutes
Rising time: 40 minutes
Baking time: 15 minutes
Makes 8 rolls

1. Prepare the sponge dough in advance by mixing the water, flour, and yeast together in a small bowl, using a fork. Cover with plastic wrap and let stand at room temperature for 2 hours.

2. In the bowl of a standing electric mixer with the dough hook attached, mix the water, yeast, sponge dough, milk, and flour at low speed for 3 minutes. With the machine running, add the salt, switch to medium speed, and continue mixing for 7 minutes.

3. Place the dough in a floured bowl, cover with plastic wrap, and let rest for 40 minutes.

4. Transfer the dough to a floured work surface and flatten it out with the palm of the hand to remove air pockets (see "Punching down," page 17).

5. Using the palms of the hands, continue flattening the dough to form a 10 x 6-inch rectangle, 1 inch thick. With the long side facing the body, slice the rectangle into 6 equal portions.

6. Place on a floured kitchen towel and let rise 40 minutes.

7. In the meantime, place a square pizza stone or unglazed ceramic tiles in the bottom of the oven and preheat to 450°F. Using a pizza paddle, quickly but gently turn each piece over (in 2 batches if necessary) onto the pizza stone or tiles so that the floured side is facing up and bake for 15 minutes, or until the crust is cracked and deeply browned. The breads are ready when a knock on the bottom produces a hollow sound.

Fresh Rosemary Focaccia

In recent years focaccia has become one of the most popular additions to menus in restaurants across America. First baked in the city of Genoa in northern Italy, the original focaccia bread has undergone many a facelift. Today it can be found in many different shapes, flavors, and imaginative serving styles.

1. In the bowl of a standing electric mixer with the dough hook attached, mix the water, yeast, 1/4 cup olive oil, and flour at low speed for 3 minutes. With the machine running, add the salt, switch to medium speed, and continue to knead for 10 minutes.

2. Place the dough in a large floured bowl, cover with plastic wrap, and let rest for 1 hour.

3. Transfer the dough to a floured work surface and flatten it out with the palm of the hand to remove air pockets (see "Punching down," page 17).

4. Grease an (approximately) 12¹/2 x 15¹/2-inch baking pan with 1 tablespoon olive oil. Place the dough in the pan and flatten it out with the palm of the hand until it fits snugly.

5. Brush the top with the remaining 1 tablespoon olive oil, sprinkle with coarse salt and rosemary, and let rise until tripled in size (about 1 hour).

6. Preheat the oven to 400°F. Use your finger to make little indentations in the top of the dough (see picture).

7. Bake for 15 minutes, or until the crust is hard, shiny, and deep golden brown.

8. Remove from the oven and let cool on a wire rack.

1¹/4 cups **water**

1 tablespoon **dry yeast**

1/4 cup plus 2 tablespoons **extra-virgin olive oil**

3¹/4 cups **unbleached all-purpose flour**

2 teaspoons **salt**

1 teaspoon **coarse salt**, for garnish

1 tablespoon fresh **rosemary leaves**, for garnish

Additional **flour** for assorted tasks

Preparation time: 20 minutes
Resting time: 1 hour
Rising time: 1 hour
Baking time: 15 minutes
Makes 1 large loaf
(10–12 servings)

Olive-Oil Flatbread

This delicious bread hails from southern France, where it basks in sunlight and Mediterranean flavors. Its flavor-absorbing ability makes it a perfect bed for piquant tuna salad, grilled steak, and many other flavorful dishes.

1 cup **water**

1/4 cup **extra-virgin olive oil**

1 tablespoon **dry yeast**

3 1/2 cups **bread flour**

2 teaspoons **salt**

1 tablespoon **extra-virgin olive oil**, for brushing

Additional **flour** for assorted tasks

Preparation time: 20 minutes
Resting time: 50 minutes
Rising time: 45 minutes
Baking time: 20 minutes
Makes 3 small loaves
or 1 large loaf
(10–12 servings)

1. In the bowl of a standing electric mixer with the dough hook attached, mix the water, 1/4 cup olive oil, yeast, and flour at low speed for 3 minutes. With the machine running, add the salt and continue to knead at low speed for 10 minutes.

2. Place the dough in a large floured bowl, cover with plastic wrap, and let rest for 50 minutes.

3. Transfer the dough to a floured work surface and flatten it out with the palm of the hand to remove air pockets (see "Punching down," page 17).

4. Divide the dough into 3 equal pieces and roll each piece into a ball. Use a lightly floured rolling pin to make three 5-inch circles, each 1/2 inch thick, and place on a large parchment paper–lined cookie sheet. Let rise 45 minutes.

5. Preheat the oven to 400ºF. Just before baking, brush each bread with olive oil, then bake for 20 minutes, or until deep brown.

NOTE: May be partially baked before freezing. Defrost and bake immediately, according to recipe directions.

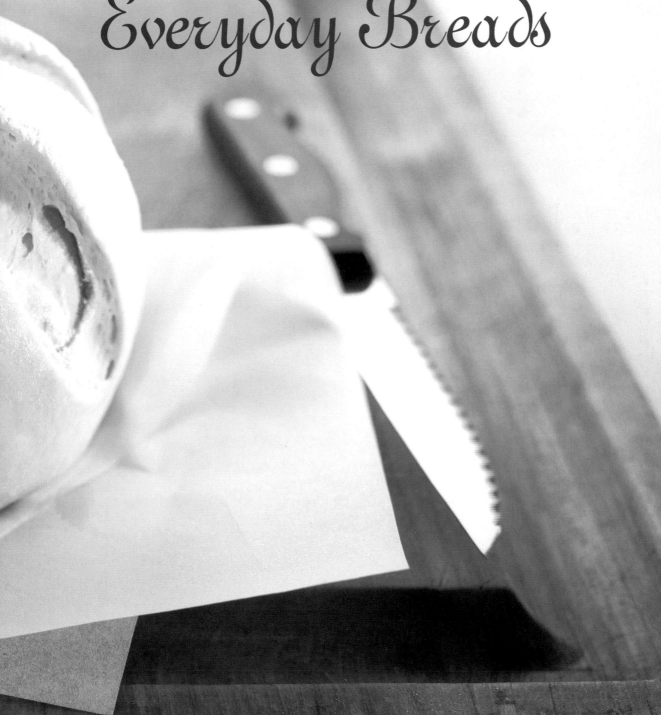

Everyday Breads

Whole Wheat Bran Bread

If you find most whole wheat breads too heavy in texture, you'll enjoy this lighter version that's rich in fiber and full of flavor. The secret is a unique combination of three kinds of leavening agents: sponge dough, sourdough, and yeast (for more information, see pages 12–15). For me, this is a "weekend bread" to make when I already have some sourdough starter on hand. I make the sponge dough Saturday mornings, bake the bread by noon, and use it for sandwiches and toasting throughout the weekend. Save any leftovers for preparing croutons.

FOR THE SPONGE DOUGH:

1 cup **whole wheat flour**

1/2 cup **water**

1 teaspoon **dry yeast**

FOR THE DOUGH:

3/4 cup **water**

1 tablespoon **dry yeast**

1/4 pound **ready-made sourdough starter** (page 14)

sponge dough

3/4 cup **bran**

2 1/2 cups **whole wheat flour**

2 teaspoons **salt**

water, for brushing

1/4 cup **bran**, for garnish

Additional **flour** for assorted tasks

1. Prepare the sponge dough in advance by mixing the flour, water, and yeast together in a bowl using a fork. Cover with plastic wrap and set aside for 2 hours.

2. In the bowl of a standing electric mixer with the dough hook attached, mix the water, yeast, sourdough, sponge dough, bran, and flour at low speed for 3 minutes. With the machine running, add the salt and continue to knead at low speed for 10 minutes.

3. Place the dough in a large floured bowl, cover with plastic wrap, and let rest for 1 hour.

4. Transfer the dough to a floured work surface and flatten it out with the palm of the hand to remove air pockets (see "Punching down," page 17). Divide the dough into 2 equal parts and roll each into a ball.

5. Place the palms of the hands on one of the balls and gently roll it backward and forward to form a 10-inch oval. Pinch the short ends of the oval into points (see picture), making the center of the loaf rounded. Repeat the process with the other ball of dough.

6. Carefully place each loaf on a floured kitchen towel and let rise 1 hour.

7. Place a square pizza stone or unglazed ceramic tiles in the bottom of the oven and preheat to 450°F. Just before baking, turn the loaves over and brush the tops with water. Sprinkle a little bran on top to garnish.

8. Using a sharp knife, make a 45-degree-angle slash down the center of each loaf (see "The Baker's Mark, page 16). Use a wooden pizza paddle to place the loaves 1 inch apart on the stone or tiles and bake for 30 minutes. The breads are ready when a knock on the bottom produces a hollow sound.

Preparation time for the
sponge dough: 2 hours
Preparation time for the
bread: 20 minutes
Resting time: 1 hour
Rising time: 1 hour
Baking time: 30 minutes
Makes 2 loaves
(each 18 slices)

Country-Style White Bread

Originally from the Brittany region of France, this bread was traditionally baked in a stone oven, which gave it a unique taste and texture. The loaf stays fresh for 2 days, and if there are any leftovers the deliciously thick crust and airy interior make for a perfect bruschetta.

FOR THE SPONGE DOUGH:

1 cup **flour**

½ cup **water**

½ teaspoon **dry yeast**

FOR THE DOUGH:

1 ¼ cups **water**

1 tablespoon **dry yeast**

3 cups **bread flour**

2 teaspoons **salt**

Additional **flour** for assorted tasks

1. Prepare the sponge dough in advance by mixing the ingredients together in a small bowl using a fork. Cover with plastic wrap and set aside for 2 hours.

2. In the bowl of a standing electric mixer with the dough hook attached, mix the sponge dough, water, yeast, and flour for 3 minutes at low speed. Add the salt, switch to medium speed, and continue to knead for another 12 minutes.

3. Place the dough in a large floured bowl, cover with a kitchen towel, and let rest at room temperature for 1 hour, or until the dough has doubled in size.

4. Transfer the dough to a floured work surface and flatten it out with the palm of the hand to remove air pockets (see "Punching down," page 17). Divide the dough into 2 equal pieces and roll each into a ball.

5. Place the palms of both hands on one of the balls of dough and roll it backward and forward until it is 14 inches long. Join the ends of the dough together to form a circle, pinching the top edges together but leaving a slit at the bottom. Repeat with the other ball of dough.

6. Line a tray with a floured kitchen towel and place the breads on top. Let rise 1 hour, or until doubled in size.

7. Place a square pizza stone or unglazed ceramic tiles in the bottom of the oven and preheat to 450°F. Using a pizza paddle, carefully place the breads on the stone or tiles and bake for 30 minutes, or until a knock on the bottom produces a hollow sound.

NOTE: If you own a convection oven, make sure to use the nonconvection setting for baking this bread.

Preparation time for the sponge dough: 2 hours
Preparation time for the dough: 20 minutes
Resting time: 1 hour
Rising time: 1 hour
Baking time: 30 minutes
Makes 2 loaves
(each 18–20 slices)

Organic Sourdough Bread

This tasty bread will keep fresh for several days.

1. In the bowl of a standing electric mixer with the dough hook attached, mix the water, sourdough, flour, wheat germ, and salt at low speed for 12 minutes.

2. Place the dough in a large floured bowl and cover with plastic wrap. Let rest for 1½ hours.

3. Transfer the dough to a floured work surface and flatten it out with the palm of the hand to remove air pockets (see "Punching down," page 17). To shape the dough, roll it into a neat ball. (The bottom of the ball will be smoother than the top.)

4. Line a large, wide bowl with a well-floured kitchen towel and place the dough inside. Let rise for 6 to 7 hours at room temperature, until tripled in size.

5. Turn the loaf out on a floured work surface and slash the top twice lengthwise and twice crosswise (see picture 3, page 16).

6. Place a 15-inch round or square pizza stone or unglazed ceramic tiles on the bottom of the oven and preheat to 450ºF. Use a pizza paddle to transfer the loaf to the oven and bake directly on the stone or tiles for 1 hour, or until a knock on the bottom of the bread produces a hollow sound.

1²/₃ cups **water**

½ pound **sourdough starter** (see page 14)

4½ cups **organic white flour**

2 tablespoons **wheat germ**

1½ tablespoons **salt**

Additional **flour** for assorted tasks

Preparation time: 20 minutes
Resting time: 1½ hours
Rising time: 6-7 hours
Baking time: 1 hour
Makes 1 round loaf
(each 15–16 slices)

Healthy Sourdough Seed Bread

Seeds are a treasure trove of protein and important vitamins and minerals. Flax seed has even been proven to help lower cholesterol. This splendid bread incorporates four different kinds of seeds for a guaranteed energy lift.

¼ pound **sourdough starter** (see page 14)

1½ cups **bread flour**

¾ cup **whole rye flour**

¾ cup **whole wheat flour**

1 cup plus 1 tablespoon **water**

2 tablespoons **salt**

2 tablespoons **wheat germ**

3 tablespoons **sunflower seeds**

3 tablespoons **flax seeds**

3 tablespoons **sesame seeds**

3 tablespoons **toasted sesame seeds**

2 tablespoons **pumpkin seeds**

½ cup **mixed sesame, flax, sunflower, and pumpkin seeds,** for garnish

Additional **flour** for assorted tasks

Preparation time: 20 minutes
Resting time: 2 hours
Rising time: 6–8 hours
Baking time: 1 hour
Makes 1 loaf
(8–10 slices)

1. In the bowl of a standing electric mixer with the dough hook attached, combine all the ingredients, except the ½ cup mixed seeds, and mix at low speed for 3 minutes. Increase the speed to medium and continue to knead for 15 minutes.

2. Place the dough in a large floured bowl and cover with a kitchen towel. Let rest at room temperature for 2 hours.

3. Transfer the dough to a floured work surface and flatten it out with the palm of the hand to remove air pockets (see "Punching down," page 17). Place the palms of both hands on the dough and roll it backward and forward until it is 12 inches long, highest in the center (see picture, page 18).

4. Pour the ½ cup mixed seeds onto the work surface and roll the dough in it, covering all sides and pressing gently to help the seeds adhere.

5. Turn over on a floured kitchen towel and let rise for 6 to 8 hours. (Don't worry if some of the seeds fall off.)

6. Place a 15-inch round pizza stone or unglazed ceramic tiles in the bottom of the oven and preheat to 450ºF.

7. Turn the dough floured side up and make two lengthwise slashes on top (see picture 2, page 16). Use a pizza paddle to carefully place the bread on the stone or tiles and bake for 30 minutes. The bread is ready when a knock on the bottom produces a hollow sound.

NOTE: If you own a convection oven, make sure to use the nonconvection setting for baking this bread.

Tuscan Bread

This simple, unassuming loaf is the favorite everyday bread in the Tuscany region of Italy. Low in salt and without any embellishments such as butter, olive oil, or eggs, it has a flavor that blends with any dish, especially when used to soak up the last bits of sauce. Use it for bruschetta or crostini, or for making excellent all-purpose bread crumbs.

FOR THE BIGA:

1 cup **bread flour**

1/3 cup **water**

1/2 teaspoon **dry yeast**

FOR THE DOUGH:

11/3 cups **water**

1 tablespoon **dry yeast**

11/2 cups **bread flour**

1 cup **durum flour**

1 teaspoon **salt**

Additional **flour** for assorted tasks

Preparation time for the biga:
2 hours
Preparation time for the dough:
20 minutes
Resting time: 1 hour
Rising time: 1 hour
Baking time: 30 minutes
Makes 2 loaves
(each 20–22 slices)

1. Make the biga in advance by mixing the bread flour, water, and yeast together with a fork in a medium bowl. Let rest for 2 hours.

2. In the bowl of a standing electric mixer with the dough hook attached, mix the biga, water, yeast, bread and durum flours for 3 minutes at low speed. Add the salt, switch to medium speed, and knead for an additional 12 minutes.

3. Place the dough in a large floured bowl and cover with a kitchen towel. Let rest for 1 hour, or until doubled in size.

4. Transfer the dough to a floured work surface and flatten it out with the palm of the hand to remove air pockets (see "Punching down," page 17). Divide the dough into 2 equal pieces.

5. Place the palms of both hands on one piece of dough and roll it backward and forward until it is 12 inches long with a convex top (see picture of loaf, page 18). Repeat with the remaining piece of dough.

6. Place each loaf on a floured kitchen towel and let rise for 1 hour, or until tripled in size.

7. Meanwhile, place a square pizza stone or unglazed ceramic tiles in the bottom of the oven and preheat to 450ºF. Use a pizza paddle to carefully place the breads on the stone or tiles and bake for 30 minutes, or until a knock on the bottom of the breads produces a hollow sound.

*NOTES: This bread is made with **biga**, the Italian version of the French sponge dough (see page 13). The difference is basically the amount of water added.*

If you own a convection oven, make sure to use the nonconvection setting for baking this bread.

Swiss Rustic Bread

I first tasted this unusual rustic bread while traveling in the towns and villages along the Swiss-German border, where it originated. Rich in dark raisins and crunchy hazelnuts, it is served fresh at breakfast with lots of butter, or it is toasted to serve as an accompaniment to ripe cheeses.

1¼ cups **water**

3 ounces **fresh yeast** or
2 tablespoons **dry yeast**

¼ pound **sourdough starter** (see page 14)

1¼ cups **bread flour**

1⅓ cups **whole rye flour**

½ cup plus 2 tablespoons **whole wheat flour**

¾ cup **dark raisins**

¾ cup peeled and toasted **hazelnuts**

2 teaspoons **salt**

Additional **flour** for assorted tasks

> **Preparation time: 20 minutes**
> **Resting time: 1 hour**
> **Rising time: 1 hour**
> **Baking time: 30 minutes**
> **Makes 2 loaves**
> **(each 18–20 slices)**

1. In the bowl of a standing electric mixer with the dough hook attached, mix the water, yeast, sourdough, flours, raisins, and hazelnuts for 3 minutes at low speed. With the machine running, add the salt, switch to medium speed, and knead an additional 8 minutes.

2. Place the dough in a large floured bowl and cover with a kitchen towel. Let rest at room temperature for 1 hour, or until the dough has doubled in size.

3. Transfer the dough to a floured work surface and flatten it out with the palm of the hand to remove air pockets (see "Punching down," page 17). Divide the dough into 2 equal pieces and roll each into a ball.

4. Place the palms of both hands on one of the balls of dough and roll it backward and forward until it is a 10-inch-long oval with a rounded center. Pinch the short edges together to create points on either side. Repeat with the remaining piece of dough.

5. Turn over each loaf and place facedown on a floured kitchen towel. Let rise for 1 hour.

6. Place a square pizza stone or unglazed ceramic tiles in the bottom of the oven and preheat to 425°F.

7. Carefully turn the loaves over. Holding a knife at a 45-degree angle to the bread, make 2 slashes on top of each loaf (for more on slashing, see "The Baker's Mark," page 16).

8. Use a pizza paddle to transfer the breads to the stone or tiles and bake for 30 minutes. The breads are ready when a knock on the bottom produces a hollow sound.

Real Jewish Rye Bread

Some people call this "real Jewish rye" because it has been a classic bread of the Eastern European Jewish kitchen for hundreds of years. It is still sold in delis today. Made with rye flour, sourdough, and caraway seeds, this heart-shaped version has a distinctive taste with lots of character that gets even better the next day.

1. In the bowl of a standing electric mixer with the dough hook attached, mix the water, yeast, sourdough, caraway seeds, and flours for 3 minutes at low speed. With the machine running, add the salt, switch to medium speed, and knead an additional 8 minutes.

2. Place the dough in a large floured bowl and cover with a kitchen towel. Let rest at room temperature for 1 hour, or until the dough has doubled in size.

3. Transfer the dough to a floured work surface and flatten it out with the palm of the hand to remove air pockets (see "Punching down," page 17). Divide the dough into 2 equal pieces. Roll each into a ball and let stand on the floured surface for 5 minutes.

4. Using a lightly floured rolling pin, roll each ball into an 8-inch circle. Fold opposite edges of the circle over toward the center, then fold the bottom edge up to form a triangle. Repeat with the other ball.

5. Line a baking sheet with parchment paper and place the triangles on it with the folded sides facing down. Use the fingers to pinch each triangle into a heart-shaped loaf. Let rise for 1 hour.

6. Preheat the oven to 425°F. Bake the hearts for 30 minutes, or until a knock on the bottom produces a hollow sound.

1¼ cups **water**

1 tablespoon **dry yeast**

¼ pound **sourdough starter** (see page 14)

⅔ cup **caraway seeds**

2½ cups **bread flour**

1 cup **whole rye flour**

2 teaspoons **salt**

Additional **flour** for assorted tasks

Preparation time: 20 minutes
Resting time: 1 hour
Rising time: 1 hour
Baking time: 30 minutes
Makes 2 loaves
(each 18–20 slices)

*NOTES: For best results, use sourdough starter made with a piece of **German Sourdough Bread** (page 108) after the first rising, or ¼ pound **Fermented Dough** (page 12) made with whole wheat flour.*

If you own a convection oven, make sure to use the nonconvection setting for baking this bread.

High-Fiber Bread

Nutritionists tell us that one of the basic elements of a healthy diet is plenty of fiber. This bread is not only rich in fiber but also contains a wealth of vitamins and minerals.

1¼ cups **water**

1 tablespoon **dry yeast**

¼ cup **wheat germ**

½ cup **bran**

½ cup **rolled oats**

½ cup **barley flour** (available in health food stores)

2½ cups **bread flour**

1 tablespoon **salt**

Additional **flour** for assorted tasks

Additional **oats for garnish**

Preparation time: 20 minutes
Resting time: 1 hour
Rising time: 1 hour
Baking time: 30 minutes
Makes 2 loaves
(each 18–20 slices)

1. In the bowl of a standing electric mixer with the dough hook attached, mix the water, yeast, wheat germ, bran, oats, and flours for 3 minutes at low speed. With the machine running, add the salt, switch to medium speed, and knead an additional 8 minutes.

2. Place the dough in a large floured bowl and cover with plastic wrap. Let rest at room temperature for 1 hour, or until the dough has doubled in size.

3. Transfer the dough to a floured work surface and flatten it out with the palm of the hand to remove air pockets (see "Punching down," page 17). Divide the dough into 2 equal pieces. Roll each into a ball and let stand on the floured surface for 5 minutes.

4. Place the palms of both hands on one of the dough pieces and roll it backward and forward until it is 12 inches long with a raised center. Sprinkle the top with oats and press them in lightly. Repeat with the other piece of dough.

5. Place each loaf on a floured kitchen towel and let rise for 1 hour.

6. Place a square pizza stone or unglazed ceramic tiles in the bottom of the oven and preheat to 450ºF. Use a pizza paddle to transfer the breads to the stone or tiles. Bake for 30 minutes, or until a knock on the bottom produces a hollow sound.

My Favorite Sourdough White Bread

Not only does this bread stay fresh for up to 2 days, it also makes great toast or bruschetta thereafter. I sometimes make this same recipe with wine substituted for the water.

1. Combine the water and sourdough in the bowl of a standing electric mixer with the dough hook attached, then add the flour and salt. Mix at low speed for 5 minutes, then switch to medium speed and knead an additional 7 minutes.

2. Place the dough in a large floured bowl and cover with plastic wrap. Let rest at room temperature for $1^1/_2$ hours.

3. Transfer the dough to a floured work surface and flatten it out with the palm of the hand to remove air pockets (see "Punching down," page 17).

4. Place the palms of both hands on the dough and roll it around until it forms a neat ball. (The bottom will usually be smoother than the top.)

5. Line a large, wide bowl with a well-floured kitchen towel and place the dough inside, with the bottom or smoother side facedown. Let rise for 6 to 7 hours, or until the dough has tripled in size.

6. Turn over on a floured surface so that the top is now facing downward. Using a sharp knife, make 7 slashes starting from the center of the round and working outward to within 2 inches from the edges, somewhat like the rays of the sun (see picture). These slashes are not just decorative, they are important to successful baking of the bread.

7. Place a round or square pizza stone or unglazed ceramic tiles in the bottom of the oven and preheat to 450°F. Use a pizza paddle to slide the bread onto the stone or tiles with the slashes facing up. Bake for 1 hour, or until a knock on the bottom of the bread produces a hollow sound.

NOTE: If you own a convection oven, make sure to use the nonconvection setting for baking this bread.

$1^2/_3$ cups **water**

1/2 pound **sourdough starter** (see page 14)

$4^1/_2$ cups **bread flour**

$1^1/_2$ tablespoons **salt**

Additional **flour** for assorted tasks

Preparation time: 20 minutes
Resting time: $1^1/_2$ hours
Rising time: 6–7 hours
Baking time: 1 hour
Makes 1 large loaf
(20–22 slices)

Poilane's Famous Country-Style Sourdough Bread

This bread was made famous by the renowned French baker Lionel Poilane, who made it one of his lifelong goals to reacquaint the French with their centuries-old tradition of eating sourdough-based breads.

1²/3 cups **water**

1/2 pound **sourdough starter** (see page 14)

2 cups **bread flour**

1³/4 cups **whole rye flour**

3/4 cup **whole wheat flour**

1¹/2 tablespoons **salt**

Additional **flour** for assorted tasks

Preparation time: 20 minutes
Resting time: 1¹/2 hours
Rising time: 6–7 hours
Baking time: 1 hour
Makes 1 loaf
(18 slices)

1. Combine the water and sourdough in the bowl of a standing electric mixer with the dough hook attached, then add the flours and salt. Mix at low speed for 12 minutes.

2. Place the dough in a large floured bowl and cover with plastic wrap. Let rest at room temperature for 1 1/2 hours.

3. Transfer the dough to a floured work surface and flatten it out with the palm of the hand to remove air pockets (see "Punching down," page 17).

4. Place the palms of both hands on the dough and roll it around until it forms a neat ball. (The bottom will usually be smoother than the top.)

5. Line a large, wide bowl with a well-floured kitchen towel and place the dough inside, with the bottom or smoother side facing down. Let rise for 6 to 7 hours, or until tripled in size.

6. Place a 15-inch square pizza stone or ceramic tiles in the bottom of the oven and preheat to 450°F.

7. Transfer the dough to a floured work surface, with the top facing up. Cut an S-shaped slash in the center of the bread (see picture). Use a pizza paddle to place the dough on the stone or tiles, and bake for 1 hour. The bread is ready when a knock on the bottom produces a hollow sound.

NOTE: *If you own a convection oven, make sure to use the nonconvection setting for baking this bread.*

German Sourdough Bread

Dark and dense, this long-lasting bread is perfect to serve with winter soups and stews. After the first rising, I always save a 1/4-pound piece of the dough to replenish my sourdough starter; this "dark" starter is perfect for making Real Jewish Rye Bread (page 101).

1¾ cups **water**

½ pound **sourdough starter** (see page 14)

1½ cups **bread flour**

1½ cups **whole rye flour**

1½ cups **whole wheat flour**

1½ tablespoons **salt**

Additional **flour** for assorted tasks

Preparation time: 20 minutes
Resting time: 1½ hours
Rising time: 6-7 hours
Baking time: 1 hour
Makes 1 loaf
(16–18 slices)

1. Combine the water and sourdough in the bowl of a standing electric mixer with the dough hook attached, then add the flours and salt. Mix at low speed for 12 minutes.

2. Place the dough in a large floured bowl and cover with plastic wrap. Let rest at room temperature for 1½ hours.

3. Transfer the dough to a floured work surface and flatten it out with the palm of the hand to remove air pockets (see "Punching down," page 17). Roll the dough into a neat ball. (The bottom will usually be smoother than the top.)

4. Line a large, wide bowl with a well-floured kitchen towel and place the loaf inside, with the bottom or smoother side facing down. Let rise for 6 to 7 hours until tripled in size.

5. Transfer the dough to a floured surface, with the smoother (floured) side still facing down. Using a sharp knife, make crisscross slashes on the top (see "The Baker's Mark," page 16).

6. Place a 15-inch round pizza stone or unglazed ceramic tiles in the bottom of the oven and preheat to 450°F. Use a pizza paddle to carefully place the dough on the stone or tiles and bake for 1 hour, or until a knock on the bottom of the bread produces a hollow sound.

NOTE: *If you own a convection oven, make sure to use the nonconvection setting for baking this bread.*

TIP: *When making sourdough bread, always save about 1/4 pound of the dough (after it has risen) to replenish sourdough starters. The piece can always be frozen for up to one month. Defrost at room temperature before using.*

Swiss Sourdough Rye

Like German Sourdough Bread, this bread is especially good with hearty winter dishes, but I also love to serve it slathered in butter alongside a platter of oysters.

1. In the bowl of a standing electric mixer with the dough hook attached, mix the water, sourdough, rye flour, and salt at low speed for 13 minutes.

2. Place the dough on a floured surface and divide into 2 equal pieces. Roll each into a neat ball. Use the palm of the hand to flatten one of the balls into (approximately) a 10-inch circle that is 1 inch thick. Repeat with the other ball.

3. Place each circle on a floured kitchen towel and let rise 4 to 5 hours, or until the circle rises and cracks on top.

4. Place a 15-inch square pizza stone or unglazed ceramic tiles in the bottom of the oven and preheat to 425°F. Use a pizza paddle to carefully transfer the circles to the stone or tiles. Bake for 40 minutes, or until a knock on the bottom of the breads produces a hollow sound.

1¼ cups **water**

½ pound **sourdough starter** (see page 14)

3½ cups **whole rye flour**

1 tablespoon **salt**

Additional **flour** for assorted tasks

Preparation time: 20 minutes
Rising time: 4–5 hours
Baking time: 40 minutes
Makes 2 loaves
(each 12–14 slices)

Gourmet Whole Wheat Sourdough Bread

This deluxe whole wheat bread is wonderful served with ripe cheeses, goat cheeses, terrines, fois gras, and premium meats.

1. In the bowl of a standing electric mixer with the dough hook attached, mix the water, yeast, sourdough, flour, and oats at low speed for 3 minutes. While the machine is running, switch the speed to medium, add the salt, and continue to knead for 10 minutes.

2. Place the dough in a large floured bowl and cover with plastic wrap. Let rest at room temperature for 1 hour.

3. Transfer the dough to a floured work surface and flatten it out with the palm of the hand to remove air pockets (see "Punching down," page 17).

4. Divide the dough into 2 equal pieces and roll each piece into a ball. (The bottom will usually be smoother than the top.) Place each on a floured kitchen towel and let rise 1 hour.

5. Place a 15-inch square pizza stone or unglazed ceramic tiles in the bottom of the oven and preheat to 450°F. Turn one loaf at a time over onto a pizza paddle so that the floured bottom is now on top. Slip the loaves into the oven and bake directly on the stone or tiles for 30 minutes, or until a knock on the bottom of the loaves produces a hollow sound.

1½ cups **water**

1 tablespoon **dry yeast**

½ pound **sourdough starter** (see page 14)

2½ cups **whole wheat flour**

1 cup **rolled oats**

1 tablespoon **salt**

Additional **flour** for assorted tasks

Preparation time: 20 minutes
Resting time: 1 hour
Rising time: 1 hour
Baking time: 30 minutes
Makes 2 loaves
(each 8–10 slices)

Festive Breads

Challah

There are countless varieties of challah, the traditional Jewish bread served on the Sabbath and for all festive occasions. This is my own version, enough for 2 loaves (also a Sabbath tradition), but you can freeze half or all the dough for up to 3 weeks just after kneading.

1. In the bowl of a standing electric mixer with the dough hook attached, mix the water, yeast, milk, egg, sugar, butter, and flour for 3 minutes at low speed. With the machine running, add the salt, switch to medium speed, and knead an additional 8 minutes. (The dough may be wrapped in plastic wrap and frozen at this point, if desired.)

2. Place the dough in a large floured bowl and cover with plastic wrap. Let rest for 1 hour. (If using frozen dough, defrost at room temperature, and let rise until doubled in size. Flatten it out to stop the rising process and divide the dough as indicated below.)

3. Transfer the dough to a floured work surface and flatten it out with the palm of the hand to remove air pockets (see "Punching down," page 17). Divide the dough into 6 equal pieces and roll each piece into a ball. Let the balls of dough rest on the floured work surface for 5 minutes.

4. Place the palms of the hands on one ball and roll it backward and forward until it is a 15-inch-long rope with slightly tapered edges. Repeat with the other dough pieces.

5. Fasten the top ends of three of the dough ropes together with a pinch. Pass the left-hand piece over the middle rope and then bring the right-hand piece over, continuing until there is no more dough left to braid. Pinch the ends together at the bottom. Repeat the process with the other 3 ropes.

6. Line 2 baking sheets with parchment paper and place a challah on each. Brush with beaten egg and sprinkle the sesame seeds on top. Let rise for 1 1/2 hours. The challah should triple in size.

7. Toward the end of rising, preheat the oven to 375ºF. Bake the challahs for 30 minutes, or until golden brown and shiny. Let cool on a wire rack for 30 minutes before serving.

1/3 cup **water**

1 tablespoon **dry yeast**

1/2 cup **cold milk**

1 large **egg**

1/2 cup **sugar**

1/4 cup **butter**, room temperature

3 1/2 cups **unbleached all-purpose flour**

2 teaspoons **salt**

1 **egg**, beaten, for brushing

1/3 cup **sesame seeds**, for garnish

Additional **flour** for assorted tasks

Preparation time: 20 minutes
Resting time: 1 hour
Rising time: 1 1/2 hours
Baking time: 30 minutes
Makes 2 loaves
(each 12–14 slices)

Fennel Seed Bread

This fennel-scented bread is magnificent with Mediterranean food, boulliabaisse, and Greek appetizers. In folk medicine, tea made of fennel seeds is considered a digestive aid.

1¼ cups **water**

1 tablespoon **dry yeast**

¼ pound **sourdough starter** (see page 14)

4 tablespoons **fennel seeds**

2½ cups **bread flour**

1 cup **whole rye flour**

2 teaspoons **salt**

Additional **flour** for assorted tasks

Preparation time: 20 minutes
Resting time: 1 hour
Rising time: 1 hour
Baking time: 30 minutes
Makes 2 loaves
(each 12–14 slices)

1. In the bowl of a standing electric mixer with the dough hook attached, mix the water, yeast, sourdough, fennel seeds, and flours for 3 minutes at low speed. With the machine running, add the salt, switch to medium speed, and knead an additional 10 minutes.

2. Place the dough in a large floured bowl and cover with plastic wrap. Let rest for 1 hour.

3. Transfer the dough to a floured work surface and flatten it out with the palm of the hand to remove air pockets (see "Punching down," page 17). Divide the dough into 2 equal pieces and roll each piece into a ball. Let the balls of dough rest on the floured work surface for 5 minutes.

4. Place the palms of the hands on one ball and roll it backward and forward until it is 10 inches long and raised in the center. Repeat with the other piece of dough.

5. Place each shaped loaf on a floured kitchen towel and let rise for 1 hour.

6. Toward the end of rising, place a square pizza stone or unglazed ceramic tiles in the bottom of the oven and preheat to 425°F. Turn the loaves over and make 2 diagonal slashes across the top of each loaf. (For more on slashing, see "The Baker's Mark," page 16.)

7. Use a pizza paddle to carefully place the breads 1 inch apart on the stone or tiles and bake for 30 minutes, or until a knock on the bottom of the breads produces a hollow sound.

Tomato-Basil Bread

This bread is great as an accompanient to Italian-style dinners or as a change-of-pace sandwich bread. I prefer to use fresh tomatoes, since red, ripe, flavorful tomatoes produce the most satisfying results. In the off-season use canned plum tomatoes. For a piquant touch, add a few finely chopped, oil-packed sun-dried tomatoes as well.

3/4 cup **water**

1 tablespoon **dry yeast**

2/3 cup **tomatoes, peeled and crushed** (or use canned)

2 tablespoons **extra-virgin olive oil**

3 1/2 cups **bread flour**

25 large **fresh basil leaves,** rinsed, dried, and stems removed

2 teaspoons **salt**

Additional **flour** for assorted tasks

Preparation time: 20 minutes
Resting time: 1 hour
Rising time: 1 hour
Baking time: 30 minutes
Makes 2 loaves
(each 12–14 slices)

---

1. In the bowl of a standing electric mixer with the dough hook attached, mix the water, yeast, tomatoes, olive oil, flour, and basil leaves for 3 minutes at low speed. With the machine running, add the salt, switch to medium speed, and knead an additional 10 minutes.

2. Place the dough in a large floured bowl and cover with plastic wrap. Let rest for 1 hour.

3. Transfer the dough to a floured work surface and flatten it out with the palm of the hand to remove air pockets (see "Punching down," page 17). Divide the dough into 2 equal pieces and roll each piece into a ball. Let the balls of dough rest on the floured work surface for 5 minutes.

4. Place the palms of the hands on one of the balls of dough and gently roll it backward and forward to form a 10-inch-long loaf with a raised center. Repeat with the other ball of dough.

5. Place each loaf on a floured kitchen towel and let rise for 1 hour.

6. Towards the end of rising, place a square pizza stone or unglazed ceramic tiles in the bottom of the oven and preheat to 425ºF. Use a pizza paddle to slip the breads onto the stone or tiles with and bake for 30 minutes. The breads are done when a knock on the bottom produces a hollow sound.

Onion Bread

If you're setting a festive buffet table with assorted cheeses, smoked meats, or fish, you'll definitely want this bread on your menu. I also forgo bagels and enjoy it with plain cream cheese and lox!

1¼ cups **water**

1 tablespoon **dry yeast**

¼ pound **sourdough starter** (see page 14)

1 cup **whole rye flour**

2½ cups **bread flour**

¾ cup **dehydrated onion flakes**

2 teaspoons **salt**

2 tablespoons **water**, for brushing

2–3 tablespoons **dehydrated onion flakes**, for garnish

Additional **flour** for assorted tasks

Preparation time: 20 minutes
Resting time: 1 hour
Rising time: 1 hour
Baking time: 30 minutes
Makes 2 loaves
(each 10–12 slices)

1. In the bowl of a standing electric mixer with the dough hook attached, mix the water, yeast, sourdough, flours, and onion flakes together for 3 minutes at low speed. With the machine running, add the salt, switch to medium speed, and knead the dough an additional 10 minutes.

2. Place the dough in a large floured bowl and cover with a kitchen towel. Let rest for 1 hour.

3. Transfer the dough to a floured work surface and flatten it out with the palm of the hand to remove air pockets (see "Punching down," page 17). Divide the dough into 2 equal pieces and roll each piece into a ball.

4. Place the palms of the hand on one ball and roll it backward and forward until it is a 10-inch-long loaf, raised in the center. Repeat with the other ball of dough.

5. Place each loaf on a floured kitchen towel and let rise for 1 hour.

6. Toward the end of rising, place a square pizza stone or unglazed ceramic tiles in the bottom of the oven and preheat to 450°F.

7. Turn over one loaf at a time onto a pizza paddle and brush the flat side (the side that was touching the towel) with 1 tablespoon water, then sprinkle with half the onion. Repeat with the second loaf.

8. Using a razor blade or sharp knife, make a diagonal slash along the length of each bread. (For more on slashing, see "The Baker's Mark," page 16.)

9. Place the breads 3 inches apart on the pizza stone or unglazed ceramic tiles and bake for 30 minutes, or until a knock on the bottom of the breads produces a hollow sound.

Pumpkin Bread

Made with fresh pumpkin, this bread is a sensational accompaniment to hearty autumn stews, but you can also enjoy it throughout the year by substituting butternut squash. It will stay fresh for 2 days and makes sensational toast in the days that follow. Its depth of flavor is due to the addition of fermented dough ("old dough"), for which you can find instructions on page 12.

1. In the bowl of a standing electric mixer with the dough hook attached, mix the water, yeast, pumpkin, fermented dough, and flour together for 3 minutes at low speed. With the machine running, add the salt, switch to medium speed, and knead the dough an additional 12 minutes.

2. Place the dough in a large floured bowl and cover with plastic wrap. Let rest for 1 hour.

3. Transfer the dough to a floured work surface and flatten it out with the palm of the hand to remove air pockets (see "Punching down," page 17). Divide the dough into 2 equal pieces and roll each piece into a ball.

4. Place each ball of dough on a floured kitchen towel and let rise for 1 hour.

5. Toward the end of rising, place a square pizza stone or unglazed ceramic tiles in the bottom of the oven and preheat to 425ºF.

6. Using a razor blade or a very sharp knife, make a 1/2-inch-deep, square-shaped slash on top of each bread. (For more on slashing, see "The Baker's Mark," page 16.) Use a pizza paddle to slip the loaves onto the stone or tiles. Bake for 30 minutes, or until a knock on the bottom of the loaves produces a hollow sound.

11/4 cups **water**

1 tablespoon **dry yeast**

1 cup **fresh pumpkin** or **butternut squash**, peeled and finely grated

1/4 pound **fermented dough** (see page 12)

31/2 cups **unbleached all-purpose flour**

2 teaspoons **salt**

Additional **flour** for assorted tasks

Preparation time: 20 minutes
Resting time: 1 hour
Rising time: 1 hour
Baking time: 30 minutes
Makes 2 loaves
(each 12–14 slices)

Perfectly Parmesan Bread

Delicately flavored, this unusual bread is a show stopper at every party and special gathering. Serve it with dips, cheeses, fish and seafood, meat, or salads . . . in short, anything! Toast any leftovers (doubtful) the next day.

1¼ cups **water**

1 tablespoon **dry yeast**

1 cup **parmesan cheese,** freshly grated

¼ pound **fermented dough** (see page 12)

3½ cups **bread flour**

2 teaspoons **salt**

2 tablespoons **water,** for brushing

¼–⅓ cup grated **Parmesan cheese,** for garnish

Additional **flour** for assorted tasks

1. In the bowl of a standing electric mixer with the dough hook attached, mix the water, yeast, Parmesan cheese, fermented dough, and flour together for 3 minutes at low speed. With the machine running, add the salt, switch to medium speed, and knead the dough an additional 12 minutes.

2. Place the dough in a large floured bowl and cover with a kitchen towel. Let rest for 1 hour.

3. Transfer the dough to a floured work surface and flatten it out with the palm of the hand to remove air pockets (see "Punching down," page 17). Divide the dough into 2 equal pieces and roll each piece into a ball.

4. Place each ball on a floured kitchen towel and let rise for 1 hour.

5. Toward the end of rising, place a square pizza stone or unglazed ceramic tiles in the bottom of the oven and preheat to 400ºF.

6. Brush the top of the balls with the water and sprinkle parmesan cheese on top to garnish. Use a pizza paddle to slip the loaves onto the stone or tiles and bake for 30 minutes. The breads are done when a knock on the bottom produces a hollow sound.

Preparation time: 20 minutes
Resting time: 1 hour
Rising time: 1 hour
Baking time: 30 minutes
Makes 2 loaves
(each 10–12 slices)

Garlic-Lover's Bread

Garlic is one of my favorite flavors. This garlic-lover's delight goes great with both Italian and Spanish dishes. Leftovers make superb croutons, especially suitable for winter soups, or they may be toasted and topped with a slice of ripe tomato and a sprinkling of coarse salt and olive oil, like they do in Catalonia.

1. In the bowl of a standing electric mixer with the dough hook attached, mix the water, yeast, garlic, sourdough, and flour together for 3 minutes at low speed. With the machine running, add the salt, switch to medium speed, and knead the dough an additional 12 minutes.

2. Place the dough in a large floured bowl and cover with plastic wrap. Let rest 1 hour.

3. Transfer the dough to a floured work surface and flatten it out with the palm of the hand to remove air pockets (see "Punching down," page 17). Divide the dough into 2 equal pieces and roll each into a ball.

4. Place the palms of the hands on one ball and roll it backward and forward to form a 10-inch-long loaf with a raised top. Repeat with the other ball.

5. Place each loaf on a floured kitchen towel and let rise for 1 hour.

6. Toward the end of rising, preheat the oven to 425°F. Just before baking, use a sharp knife or razor blade to make a long diagonal slash down the center of the breads. (For more on slashing, see "The Baker's Mark," page 16.)

7. Place the breads 3 inches apart on a parchment paper–lined baking sheet and bake for 30 minutes, or until a knock on the bottom of the loaves produces a hollow sound.

1¼ cups **water**

1 tablespoon **dry yeast**

15 **garlic cloves**, crushed

¼ pound **sourdough starter** (see page 14)

3½ cups **bread flour**

2 teaspoons **salt**

Additional **flour** for assorted tasks

Preparation time: 20 minutes
Resting time: 1 hour
Rising time: 1 hour
Baking time: 30 minutes
Makes 2 loaves
(each 10–12 slices)

Bacon Bread

There are many versions of bacon bread, but this one comes to us from Alsace on the French-German border, where it is often served with hearty dishes like choucroute or pâté.
It tastes wonderful toasted.

1. In the bowl of a standing electric mixer with the dough hook attached, mix the water, yeast, diced bacon, sourdough, and flour for 3 minutes at low speed. With the machine running, add the salt, switch to medium speed, and knead an additional 13 minutes.

2. Place the dough in a large floured bowl and cover with a kitchen towel. Let rest for 1 hour.

3. Transfer the dough to a floured work surface and flatten it out with the palm of the hand to remove air pockets (see "Punching down," page 17). Divide the dough into 2 equal pieces.

4. Place the palms of the hands on one ball and roll it backward and forward to form a 10-inch-long loaf with a raised center. Repeat with the other ball.

5. Place each loaf on a floured kitchen towel and let rise for 1 hour.

6. Toward the end of rising, place a square pizza stone or unglazed ceramic tiles in the bottom of the oven and preheat to 400ºF. Using a pizza paddle, carefully place the loaves 3 inches apart on the stone or tiles and bake for 30 minutes, or until a knock on the bottom of the loaves produces a hollow sound.

1¼ cups **water**

1 tablespoon **dry yeast**

¾ pound **slab bacon**, finely diced

¼ pound **sourdough starter** (see page 14)

3½ cups **unbleached all-purpose flour**

2 teaspoons **salt**

Additional **flour** for assorted tasks

Preparation time: 20 minutes
Resting time: 1 hour
Rising time: 1 hour
Baking time: 30 minutes
Makes 2 loaves
(each 9–10 slices)

Corn Bread

Leavened with both yeast and sourdough, this bread puts a whole new spin on the traditional corn bread. Its crispy crust and rich corn flavor make it eminently suitable to accompany your favorite Mexican or Creole dishes, or just serve it fresh with lots of butter.

1 cup plus 1 tablespoon **water**

2 tablespoons **dry yeast**

¼ pound **sourdough starter** (see page 14)

1½ cups **bread flour**

2 cups **cornmeal**

2 teaspoons **salt**

Additional **flour** for assorted tasks

Preparation time: 20 minutes
Resting time: 1 hour
Rising time: 1 hour
Baking time: 40 minutes
Makes 2 loaves
(each 10–12 slices)

---

1. In the bowl of a standing electric mixer with the dough hook attached, mix the water, yeast, sourdough, flour, and cornmeal for 3 minutes at low speed. With the machine running, add the salt, switch to medium speed, and knead the dough an additional 10 minutes.

2. Place the dough in a large floured bowl and cover with a kitchen towel. Let rest for 1 hour.

3. Transfer the dough to a floured work surface and flatten it out with the palm of the hand to remove air pockets (see "Punching down," page 17). Divide the dough into 2 equal pieces and roll each piece into a ball.

4. Place the palms of the hands on one ball and roll it backward and forward until it is 12 inches long and raised in the center. Repeat with the remaining ball.

5. Place each loaf on a floured kitchen towel and let rise for 1 hour.

6. Toward the end of rising, place a square pizza stone or unglazed ceramic tiles in the bottom of the oven and preheat to 400ºF.

7. Just before baking, use a razor blade or sharp knife to make a row of X-shaped slashes along the length of each bread. (For more on slashing, see "The Baker's Mark," page 16.)

8. Use a pizza paddle to help carefully place the loaves 2 inches apart on the stone or tiles and bake for 40 minutes, or until a knock on the bottom of the breads produces a hollow sound.

Pyrenees Mountain Bread

Along the fabulous Pyrenees Mountains lining the border between France and Spain this earthy bread is served in thick slices with hearty meat stews, as the base for Roquefort cheese sandwiches, and as a staple at all kinds of buffets.

1 cup plus 1 tablespoon **water**

1 tablespoon **dry yeast**

¼ pound **fermented dough** (see page 12)

2½ cups **bread flour**

¾ cup **whole rye flour**

¼ cup **wheat germ**

2 teaspoons **salt**

Additional **flour** for assorted tasks

Preparation time: 20 minutes
Resting time: 1 hour
Rising time: 1 hour
Baking time: 30 minutes
Makes 2 loaves
(each 10–12 slices)

1. In the bowl of a standing electric mixer with the dough hook attached, mix the water, yeast, fermented dough, flours, and wheat germ for 3 minutes at low speed. With the machine running, add the salt, switch to medium speed, and knead an additional 10 minutes.

2. Place the dough in a large floured bowl and cover with plastic wrap. Let rest for 1 hour.

3. Transfer the dough to a floured work surface and flatten it out with the palm of the hand to remove air pockets (see "Punching down," page 17). Divide the dough into 2 equal pieces and roll each piece into a ball.

4. Using a floured rolling pin, roll out a corner of 1 ball of dough to form a 10-inch-long, tongue-shaped piece jutting out from the round ball. Fold the "tongue" over the round ball to form a kind of cap (see picture). Repeat with the other ball of dough.

5. Place each loaf on a floured kitchen towel and let rise for 1 hour.

6. Toward the end of rising, place a pizza stone or unglazed ceramic tiles in the bottom of the oven and preheat to 450°F. Use a pizza paddle to place the loaves 4 inches apart on the stone or tiles and bake for 30 minutes, or until a knock on the bottom of the breads produces a hollow sound.

NOTE: *If you own a convection oven, make sure to use the nonconvection setting for baking this bread.*

French Olive Bread

A favorite bread in the olive-growing region of Provence, these white flour–based flatbreads are light and airy on the inside with a hard crust on the outside. At home we serve them at lunch in the garden as an accompaniment to any dish that has a rich sauce.

1. In the bowl of a standing electric mixer with the dough hook attached, mix the water, yeast, olive oil, olives, and flour together for 3 minutes at low speed. With the machine running, add the salt, switch to medium speed, and knead the dough an additional 18 minutes.

2. Place the dough in a large floured bowl and cover with plastic wrap. Let rest for 40 minutes.

3. Transfer the dough to a floured work surface and flatten it out with the palm of the hand to remove air pockets (see "Punching down," page 17). Divide the dough into 2 equal pieces and roll each piece into a ball. Let stand 5 minutes.

4. Use both hands to press one ball of the dough into a flat 8- or 9-inch circle, 1/2 inch thick. Repeat with the other ball of dough.

5. Place each circle on a floured kitchen towel and let rise for 50 minutes, or until doubled in size.

6. Toward the end of rising, place a square pizza stone or unglazed ceramic tiles in the bottom of the oven and preheat to 425°F. Use a pizza paddle to place the breads 3 inches apart on the stone or tiles and bake for 20 minutes, or until a knock on the bottom of the breads produces a hollow sound.

11/4 cups **water**

1 tablespoon **dry yeast**

2 tablespoons **extra-virgin olive oil**

1/2 cup **pitted black olives**, finely chopped

31/2 cups **unbleached all-purpose flour**

2 teaspoons **salt**

Additional **flour** for assorted tasks

Preparation time: 25 minutes
Resting time: 40 minutes
Rising time: 50 minutes
Baking time: 20 minutes
Makes 2 flatbreads
(each 6–8 slices)

Grissini

Everybody loves grissini, those light crispy bread sticks that are so great with appetizers and soups, or just to snack on all by themselves. But homemade grissini are in a class of their own. For variety, substitute chopped oil-packed sun-dried tomatoes, thyme, oregano, or olives for the rosemary.

1 cup plus 1 tablespoon **water**

1 tablespoon **dry yeast**

2 tablespoons **extra-virgin olive oil**

2 tablespoons chopped **fresh rosemary**

3½ cups **unbleached all-purpose flour**

1 tablespoon **salt**

Additional **flour** for assorted tasks

Preparation time: 20 minutes
Resting time: 40 minutes
Rising time: 50 minutes
Baking time: 15 minutes
Makes 16 bread sticks

1. In the bowl of a standing electric mixer with the dough hook attached, mix the water, yeast, olive oil, rosemary, and flour for 3 minutes at low speed. With the machine running, add the salt, switch to medium speed, and knead the dough an additional 7 minutes.

2. Place the dough in a large floured bowl and cover with plastic wrap. Let rest for 40 minutes.

3. Transfer the dough to a floured work surface and flatten it out with the palm of the hand to remove air pockets (see "Punching down," page 17). Divide the dough into 4 equal pieces, then each piece into 4 smaller pieces, for a total of 16.

4. Roll each piece into a ball and let stand on the floured surface for 5 minutes.

5. Place the palms of the hands on one ball and roll it backward and forward until it is 15 inches long. Repeat with the remaining ball.

6. Place the bread sticks 1 inch apart on a parchment paper–lined baking pan and let rise for 50 minutes.

7. Toward the end of rising, preheat the oven to 425ºF. Bake the bread sticks for 15 minutes, or until golden brown.

Favorite Beer Bread

In my seasonal kitchen this is a winter bread, wonderful with a slow-baked stew and a glass of Rioja Grande Maison Reserve. A world apart from those instant-type beer breads, my Favorite Beer Bread is leavened with sourdough, enhanced with rye, and topped with a unique mixture for the ultimate beer experience.

1. Prepare the topping in advance by mixing the ingredients in a small bowl using a fork. Cover with plastic wrap and set aside for 2 hours.

2. In the bowl of a standing electric mixer with the dough hook attached, mix the water, yeast, beer, sourdough, and flours for 3 minutes at low speed. With the machine running, add the salt, switch to medium speed, and knead the dough an additional 10 minutes.

3. Place the dough in a large floured bowl and cover with plastic wrap. Let rest for 1 hour.

4. Transfer the dough to a floured work surface and flatten it out with the palm of the hand to remove air pockets (see "Punching down," page 17). Divide the dough into 2 equal pieces and roll each piece into a ball.

5. Place the balls 2 inches apart on a parchment paper–lined baking sheet and let rise for 1 hour.

6. Use a spatula to spread the topping on the loaves.

7. Bake in a preheated 425ºF oven for 30 minutes, or until a knock on the bottom of the loaves produces a hollow sound.

FOR THE TOPPING:

1/4 cup **beer**

3 tablespoons **whole rye flour**

1/2 teaspoon **dry yeast**

1/2 teaspoon **salt**

FOR THE DOUGH:

3/4 cup **water**

1 tablespoon **dry yeast**

1/2 cup **beer**

1/2 pound **sourdough starter** (see page 14)

2 1/2 cups **bread flour**

1 cup **whole rye flour**

2 teaspoons **salt**

Additional **flour** for assorted tasks

Topping resting time: 2 hours
Preparation time: 20 minutes
Resting time: 1 hour
Rising time: 1 hour
Baking time: 30 minutes
Makes 2 loaves
(each 8–10 slices)

Irish Potato Bread

This classic Irish potato bread is light and airy with a thick crust. It's a natural accompaniment to any sauce or gravy.

1¼ cups **water**

1 tablespoon **dry yeast**

1 tablespoon **sugar**

½ cup boiled and mashed **potatoes**

3½ cups **bread flour**

2 teaspoons **salt**

Additional **flour** for assorted tasks

Preparation time: 20 minutes
Resting time: 1 hour
Rising time: 50 minutes
Baking time: 30 minutes
Makes 2 loaves
(each 8–10 slices)

1. In the bowl of a standing electric mixer with the dough hook attached, mix the water, yeast, sugar, mashed potatoes, and flour for 3 minutes at low speed. With the machine running, add the salt, switch to medium speed, and knead the dough an additional 6 minutes.

2. Place the dough in a large floured bowl and cover with a kitchen towel. Let rest for 1 hour.

3. Transfer the dough to a floured work surface and flatten it out with the palm of the hand to remove air pockets (see "Punching down," page 17). Divide the dough into 2 equal pieces and roll each piece into a ball.

4. Using a lightly floured rolling pin, roll each ball into a 10-inch circle, 1 inch thick. Fold the top and bottom edges inward, then the sides, to form an 8 x 8-inch rectangle.

5. Let rise on the floured work surface for 50 minutes.

6. Toward the end of rising, place a square pizza stone or unglazed ceramic tiles in the bottom of the oven and preheat to 400ºF. Use a pizza paddle to slip the breads onto the stone or tiles and bake for 30 minutes. The breads are done when a knock on the bottom produces a hollow sound.

Decorative Breads

*Here's the recipe for those festive, edible bread dough decorations that allow you to adorn tables and buffets with lovely breads, just like the professionals do. Once you learn the basic technique it's fun to create your own designs. At home these bread creations will stay fresh at least 1 week and can be frozen for up to 1 month, if desired. To use, just defrost and "stick" to the bread according to directions. I use these decorations only on **Organic Sourdough Bread** (page 93), **My Favorite Sourdough White Bread** (page 105) and **German Sourdough Bread** (page 108).*

1. In the bowl of a standing electric mixer with the dough hook attached, combine all the ingredients except 1 tablespoon water and mix for 3 minutes on low speed. Switch the speed to medium and continue to knead for 6 minutes.

2. Cover with plastic wrap and place in the refrigerator. Let rest 1 hour.

3. On a floured work surface, using a lightly floured rolling pin, roll out the dough to a thickness of 1/4 inch.

4. Use cookie cutters, stencils, or a single-edge razor to cut out desired shapes from the dough.

5. Place the risen bread dough loaf on a floured surface, with the raised side facing down. Moisten the places where the decorations are to be fastened by brushing with a little water.

6. Stick the decorations on top of the loaf in the desired pattern and press lightly to fasten.

7. Bake according to the recipe directions of the specific loaf chosen.

NOTE: *It's a good idea to fully plan the design of the finished bread before starting.*

3½ cups **unbleached all-purpose flour**

1 teaspoon **salt**

3 tablespoons **vegetable oil**

¾ cup plus 1 tablespoon **water**, for brushing

Additional **flour** for assorted tasks

Preparation time: 10 minutes
Resting time: 1 hour
Makes enough to decorate
1 loaf of **Organic Sourdough Bread** (page 93),
My Favorite Sourdough White Bread (page 105), or
German Sourdough Bread (page 108)

Delectable Snacks

Preparation time:
1 hour 15 minutes
Resting time: 1 hour
Rising time: 20 minutes
Cooking time: 40–50 minutes
Baking time: 10 minutes
Makes 2 tarts
(each 4 servings)

Pissaldière

French Onion Tart

The French version of pizza, Pissaldière has an egg-based crust and various toppings, but never tomatoes and mozzarella. The dough may be prepared up to 24 hours in advance.

1. In the bowl of a standing electric mixer with the dough hook attached, mix the water, milk, yeast, sugar, olive oil, eggs, and bread flour for 3 minutes at low speed. With the machine running, add the salt, switch to medium speed, and knead an additional 10 minutes.

2. Place the dough in a large floured bowl and cover with plastic wrap. Let rest for 1 hour (or refrigerate the dough at this point for up to 24 hours).

3. Heat the olive oil for the onion topping in a large skillet, then gently sauté the onions, garlic, and thyme leaves over low heat, stirring often. Cook for 40 to 50 minutes, until the mixture has a golden hue. Remove from heat and bring to room temperature.

4. On a floured surface, divide the dough into 2 equal parts and roll each into a ball. (If using chilled dough, let rise on the floured work surface for 20 minutes before proceeding.)

5. Using a lightly floured rolling pin, roll out one ball at a time to form a 12-inch circle, 1/4 inch thick. Spread half the onion mixture, anchovy fillets, capers, and olives on each circle.

6. Place a square pizza stone or unglazed ceramic tiles in the bottom of the oven and preheat to 470ºF. Use a pizza paddle to carefully slip one tart onto the stone or tiles and bake for 10 minutes. Remove and bake the other tart.

7. Cool slightly and cut each tart into 4 wedges to serve.

FOR THE DOUGH:

1/3 cup **water**

1/4 cup **cold milk**

1 tablespoon **dry yeast**

4 teaspoons **sugar**

2 tablespoons **extra-virgin olive oil**

2 large **eggs**

3 cups **bread flour**

2 teaspoons **salt**

Additional **flour** for assorted tasks

FOR THE ONION TOPPING:

1 tablespoon **extra-virgin olive oil**

1 pound **onions,** thinly sliced

1/2 teaspoon crushed **garlic**

2 tablespoons **fresh thyme leaves**

1 ounce (about 1/2 container) **anchovy fillets in oil,** drained

1 tablespoon **capers,** drained and chopped

25 pitted **black olives**

Sfogliati al Vino Rosso
Italian Red Wine & Ham Croissants

Infused with butter and red wine, these unusual and fabulous rose-colored flaky pastries are something between a croissant and a roll. I like to bake them in the morning to take along on picnics, to serve at family dinners, or to use as a quick snack along with a glass of sparkling wine. The dough can even be frozen for up to 2 weeks.

1/2 cup **dry red wine**

1/2 cup **tomato paste**

1/3 cup **water**

1 tablespoon **dry yeast**

4 teaspooons **sugar**

1/4 cup **butter**, room temperature

3 1/2 cups **bread flour**

2 teaspoons **salt**

1/4 pound **butter**, chilled, for folding

12 very thin slices **prosciutto** or **bacon** (each about 6 inches long and 2 inches wide)

1 **egg**, beaten, for brushing

Additional **flour** for assorted tasks

Preparation time: 50 minutes
Resting time: 5 hours
Chilling time: 1 hour
Rising time: 1 1/2 hours
Baking time: 15 minutes
Makes 10–12 croissants

1. In the bowl of a standing electric mixer with the dough hook attached, mix the red wine, tomato paste, water, yeast, sugar, 1/4 cup butter, and flour for 3 minutes at low speed. With the machine running, add the salt, switch to medium speed, and knead the dough an additional 7 minutes.

2. Wrap the dough in several layers of plastic wrap. Let rest for 5 hours in the refrigerator.

3. Place the dough on a floured work surface and sprinkle a little flour on top. Using a lightly floured rolling pin, roll the dough into a 10 x 20-inch rectangle, 1/2 inch thick.

4. Wrap the 1/4 pound chilled butter with parchment paper and roll it out to a thickness of 1/4 inch. Remove the paper from the top of the butter and turn it over onto the dough. Remove the rest of the parchment paper and fold all four sides of the dough inward to cover the butter.

5. Sprinkle a little more flour on top of the dough and roll it out again to form the same size rectangle as before. Fold the long sides of the rectangle inward, then fold the rectangle in half. Wrap the dough in plastic wrap and place in the refrigerator for 30 minutes.

6. Remove the dough from the refrigerator, place on a floured work surface, and sprinkle a little flour on top. Once again, roll it into a 10 x 20-inch rectangle, 1/2 inch thick. Fold the long sides of the rectangle inward, then fold the rectangle in half, just as before.

7. Wrap the dough in plastic wrap and place in the refrigerator for another 30 minutes. (At this point the dough can be frozen for up to 2 weeks. To use, defrost at room temperature and proceed with the recipe.)

8. Using a lightly floured rolling pin, roll the dough out on a floured surface to form an 8 x 20-inch rectangle. Cut the dough into triangles with two 8-inch sides and a base of 2¹/2 inches. There should be a total of 10 to 12 triangles.

9. Place a slice of the prosciutto in the base of each triangle and roll up from the bottom to the top, like you would a croissant (see picture, page 18).

10. Arrange the croissants 3 inches apart on a parchment paper–lined baking sheet. Brush with beaten egg and let rise for 1¹/2 hours, or until doubled in size. Bake in a preheated 400ºF oven for about 15 minutes, or until reddish brown.

Bavarian Pretzel

Although doughy pretzels are originally from the Bavarian region of Germany, their texture always reminds me of the kind sold warm by street vendors in New York.

1 cup **water**

1 tablespoon **dry yeast**

3¹/₂ cups **bread flour**

1 tablespoon **vegetable oil**

2 teaspoons **salt**

1 cup **warm water** plus 2 teaspoons **baking soda**, for brushing

1 tablespoon **coarse salt**, for garnish

Additional **flour** for assorted tasks

Preparation time: 20 minutes
Resting time: 40 minutes
Rising time: 40 minutes
Baking time: 20 minutes
Makes 8 pretzels

1. In the bowl of a standing electric mixer with the dough hook attached, mix the water, yeast, and bread flour for 7 minutes at low speed. With the machine running, add the oil and 2 teaspoons salt, switch to medium speed, and knead the dough an additional 6 minutes.

2. Place the dough in a large floured bowl and cover with a kitchen towel. Let rest for 40 minutes.

3. Transfer the dough to a floured work surface and flatten it out with the palm of the hand to remove air pockets (see "Punching down," page 17). Divide the dough into 2 equal pieces, then each piece into 4 parts, for a total of 8. Let rest on the floured work surface for 5 minutes.

4. Using the palms of the hands, roll each piece into an oval. Use the fingers to work the dough at the sides of the oval into long strips, leaving the center rounded (see picture 1), for a total length of 18 inches.

5. Pick up the ends of each strip, cross them over each other to form a loop, then cross them over again and press them down on either side of the dough loop (see picture 2).

6. Arrange the pretzels 2 inches apart on a parchment paper–lined baking sheet. Let rise for 40 minutes.

7. Brush with the water–baking soda mixture and sprinkle with coarse salt. Bake in a preheated 400ºF oven for about 20 minutes, until browned but not dark. The pretzels are done when the crust is hardened.

1

2

Pizza Bianca

Many people refer to this as focaccia, but it's actually a pizza, just without the tomato sauce or cheese. You can serve it as-is for a snack or starter, or use it to make fabulous sandwiches.

1. In the bowl of a standing electric mixer with the dough hook attached, mix the water, sugar, yeast, olive oil, and flour for 5 minutes at low speed. With the machine running, add the 2 teaspoons salt, switch to medium speed, and knead the dough an additional 10 minutes.

2. Place the dough in a large floured bowl and cover with plastic wrap. Let rest for 1 hour.

3. Transfer the dough to a floured work surface and flatten it out with the palm of the hand to remove air pockets (see "Punching down," page 17). Divide the dough into 4 equal pieces and roll each into a ball.

4. Let the balls of dough rest on the floured work surface for 10 minutes. (At this point the balls may be wrapped in plastic wrap and chilled in the refrigerator for up to 24 hours.)

5. Place a square or round pizza stone or unglazed ceramic tiles in the bottom of the oven and preheat to 500°F.

6. Just before baking, use a lightly floured rolling pin to roll each ball into a 1/4-inch-thick oval shape. Use the fingertips to make indentations in the dough, as for focaccia, then sprinkle the olive oil and coarse salt on top. Add a little dried oregano too, if desired.

7. Use a pizza paddle to slip the pizzas into the oven and bake directly on the stone or tiles for 7 minutes, or until golden brown.

NOTE: If I'm having a party, I like to prepare the dough a day in advance and keep it chilled until I'm ready to use it.

1 cup **water**

2 tablespoons **sugar**

2 teaspoons **dry yeast**

1 tablespoon **extra-virgin olive oil**

3 cups **bread flour**

2 teaspoons **salt**

1 teaspoon **coarse salt** plus 2 tablespoons **extra-virgin olive oil**, for garnish

Additional **flour** for assorted tasks

Preparation time: 20 minutes
Resting time: 1 hour
Rising time: 10 minutes
Baking time: 7 minutes
Makes 4 individual pizzas

My Favorite Pizza

My family and friends are crazy about this crispy-thin pizza, baked right on the unglazed ceramic tiles in my oven (a square or round pizza stone works just as well, of course). And if you think the crust sounds good, wait until you try the no-cook pizza sauce that goes with it!

3 cups **bread flour**

½ cup **cold milk**

½ cup **water**

2 tablespoons **sugar**

2 teaspoons **dry yeast**

1 tablespoon **extra-virgin olive oil** (preferably Italian)

2 teaspoons **salt**

Perfect Pizza Tomato Sauce (recipe follows)

½ pound **mozzarella cheese**, sliced

Additional **flour** for assorted tasks

Preparation time: 30 minutes
Resting time: 1 hour
Rising time: 10 minutes
Baking time: 10 minutes
Makes 2 pizzas
(each 4 slices)
or 4 individual pizzas

1. In the bowl of a standing electric mixer with the dough hook attached, mix the flour, milk, water, sugar, yeast, and olive oil for 5 minutes at low speed. With the machine running, add the salt, switch to medium speed, and knead the dough an additional 10 minutes.

2. Place the dough in a large floured bowl and cover with plastic wrap. Let rest for 1 hour.

3. In the meantime, prepare the **Perfect Pizza Tomato Sauce** according to directions (see recipe on opposite page).

4. Transfer the dough to a floured work surface and flatten it out with the palm of the hand to remove air pockets (see "Punching down," page 17). Divide the dough into 2 equal pieces (for family-sized pizzas) or into 4 pieces (for individual pizzas). Let rise, uncovered, for 10 minutes.

5. Roll each piece into a ball on the floured work surface. (At this point the balls may be wrapped in plastic wrap and chilled in the refrigerator for up to 24 hours.) Using a floured rolling pin, roll the balls of dough into ⅛-inch-thick circles.

6. Place a round or square pizza stone or unglazed ceramic tiles in the bottom of the oven and preheat to 500°F.

7. Divide the tomato sauce between the circles and place the cheese on top. Use a pizza paddle to help slip the pizzas into the oven. (Larger pizzas may need to be baked one at a time.) Bake directly on the stone or tiles for 10 minutes, or until lightly browned and bubbly.

NOTE: The dough may be prepared up to 24 hours in advance, wrapped in plastic wrap, and chilled until ready to use.

Perfect Pizza Tomato Sauce

1. Combine all the ingredients in a blender and process until smooth.

2. Let stand at least 30 minutes before using.

3. The sauce may be frozen for up to 2 weeks. Defrost at room temperature before using.

Makes enough for 2 My Favorite Pizzas (1 recipe)

2 pounds **canned peeled whole plum tomatoes**

3 tablespoons **extra-virgin olive oil**

1 tablespoon **red wine vinegar**

2 teaspoons **salt**

1 teaspoon **black pepper**

2 tablespoons **dried oregano**

2 tablespoons **tomato paste**

Index